ULTIMATE

THE GREATEST SPORT
EVER INVENTED BY MAN

ULTIMATE

THE GREATEST SPORT EVER INVENTED BY MAN

PASQUALE
ANTHONY
LEONARDO

ART BY
CADE BEAULIEU

BREAKAWAY BOOKS
HALCOTTSVILLE, NEW YORK
2010

ULTIMATE: THE GREATEST SPORT EVER INVENTED BY MAN

COPYRIGHT 2007 by PASQUALE ANTHONY LEONARDO IV
LLUSTRATIONS COPYRIGHT 2007 BY CADE BEAULIEU

ISBN: 978-1-891369-75-9
LIBRARY OF CONGRESS CONTROL NUMBER: 2007925651

PUBLISHED BY BREAKAWAY BOOKS
P.O. BOX 24
HALCOTTSVILLE, NY 12438

WWW.BREAKAWAYBOOKS.COM

TO JANE AND THE SPUDS

ILLUSTRATIONS by Cade Beaulieu

EDITRIX: Jane Carlen

CONTRIBUTING WRITERS: Jane Carlen, Katie Derickson, Becca Tucker

CONTRIBUTORS: Evan Blumberg, Melle Clarke, Chris Cline, Jan Fuhse, PJ Wentz

PHOTOGRAPHY REFERENCES: Brian Canniff, James Tiberius Coyne, Nick Gorevic, Burt Granofsky, Pete Krautscheid, Matt Lane (see www.MattLanePhotos.com), Alex Peters

UNPROFESSIONAL MODELS: Kerry Beyrer, Jane Carlen, Matt Clark, Dan Furfari, The Gata, Sean Geran, Vale Jokisch, Anne Mercier, Lucas Murphy, Joe Nichols, Shannon O'Malley, Chris Pridgen, Amber Sinicrope, Natalya Stolichnaya, Xtehn Titcomb, Becca Tucker, Dave Wexler, Ben "Huxley" Yang

Thanks to Peter McGuigan, Tom Vacca, Bob Schlipf, Stuyvesant Sticky Fingers, Lotus Eaters, Bashing Piñatas, Smartwhore, Notre Dame Ultimate, South Bend Ultimate, Garth, Cade, Jeff, Mom, Dad, Kristin

Book design by Jeff Koyen

Cover image: Beau Kittredge is up and over Drew Mahowald at the 2006 Colorado Cup, even if it was an uncontested foul call.

Photograph by Volker Neumann

SECOND EDITION

CONTENTS

TIPS FROM THE EXPERTS

WHAT IS ULTIMATE?

Joel Silver, God of Ultimate.

Undoubtedly you've heard of Ultimate. But what is it exactly? Who plays Ultimate and why? How can an adjective be a sport? These questions and more will be answered as you read about the most misunderstood team flying disc field running sport on the planet. Welcome to *Ultimate: The Greatest Sport Ever Invented by Man.*

FREQUENTLY ASKED QUESTIONS

What is Ultimate?

Some say that Ultimate is the most misunderstood team flying disc field running sport on the planet. Most people think it's Frisbee football played barefoot and without boundaries, but those people are wrong. Ultimate is played seven-on-seven on fields 70 yards long and 40 yards wide with end zones 25 yards deep. In Ultimate, you must pass the disc (or Frisbee, *see*

TEN RESPONSES YOU'LL GET WHEN YOU TELL SOMEONE YOU PLAY ULTIMATE

1. Frisbee is a sport?
2. What do you win?
3. Do you wear tie-dyes?
4. Is it in the Olympics?
5. I have a friend named Dave who's really into that Frisbee thing. You probably know him, right?
6. I play Ultimate sometimes — it's just like golf but with a Frisbee.
7. We did Ultimate in high school gym class when we weren't playing sports.
8. I saw it on TV once and those dogs can really jump!
9. I like throwing the Frisbee when I go to the beach.
10. My college had a team and they won Ultimate.

below) from teammate to teammate until someone catches it in the end zone for a 1-point score. Games are commonly played to 15 points. Running with the disc, tackling, and jumping really high are not allowed. Unsportsmanlike play, purposeful fouling, and anything "not cool" is against Ultimate's rules regarding the Spirit of the Game.

Ultimate games are played between two teams at a time, each team consisting of five to thirty-five players, although only seven are allowed to play on the field at once. A well-played Ultimate game combines the cutting of basketball, the passing of football, the running of soccer, the unruliness of hockey, the hand-eye coordination of baseball, the foot speed of tennis, and the complete and total mind/body control of dancesport. Purists regard Ultimate as the ultimate sport.

Why do some people call it Ultimate and others Ultimate Frisbee?

The sport was originally called Ultimate Frisbee when the rules were typed in 1970. At the time the only flying discs suitable for sports were Wham-O-brand Frisbees. In 1988, however, Ultimate players voted to use Discraft-brand discs for official play. Wham-O protected its trademark on the word *Frisbee,* and so Ultimate stopped using the term *Ultimate Frisbee.*

Ultimate Frisbee is still used informally, however, because calling a sport Ultimate can sometimes cry out for mockery.

POPULAR CITIES IN NORTH AMERICA WHERE YOU CAN PLAY ULTIMATE WITHOUT BEING MOCKED

OTTAWA, ONTARIO. Largest summer league ever built by mankind.

PHILADELPHIA, PENNSYLVANIA. There are some real good parties at Edgely Fields after PADA games.

MADISON, WISCONSIN; ANN ARBOR, MICHIGAN and AUSTIN, TEXAS. Giant state schools in left-leaning college towns provide the players and free time perfect for alterna-sports like Ultimate.

RALEIGH-DURHAM, NORTH CAROLINA. Ken Dobyns used to live near here.

BOULDER, COLORADO. Fact: mountains make one a better person.

BAY AREA, CALIFORNIA. Includes Oakland, San Francisco, San Jose, Santa Cruz, Palo Alto, and that one hippie spot in Golden Gate park.

BOSTON, MASSACHUSETTS. The question in Boston is when do they stop playing Ultimate? Party scene is mediocre, however.

SAN DIEGO, CALIFORNIA. But only if you play Goaltimate.

GAINESVILLE, FLORIDA. Local cow patches good for growing psilocybin mushrooms which in turn are good for growing long hair.

ATLANTA, GEORGIA. Fact: Georgia's on my mind, and so is Magic City.

WASHINGTON DC. All those post-college public-sector workers like to geek out in the WAFC summer league.

CHICAGO, ILLINOIS. Chicago is a hip, progressive, quasi-European old city which appreciates what the kids are doing.

TORONTO, ONTARIO. Toronto is a hip, progressive, quasi-Chicagoan old city which appreciates what the kids are doing.

VANCOUVER, BRITISH COLUMBIA. You can ski, hike, medicate for glaucoma, and play tons of Ultimate.

BROOKLYN, NEW YORK. Honestly—you could play polo with water buffaloes in in Brooklyn's Prospect Park and no one would mind.

MONTRÉAL, QUÉBEC. Indoor in the winter, hyperactive in summer.

MINNEAPOLIS, MINNESOTA. This city is addicted to Ultimate and needs a 12-step program in order to quit.

PORTLAND, OREGON. Ultimate helps keep Portland weird.

SEATTLE, WASHINGTON. Epicenter of Ultimate chic for the athletic set. No one dares make fun of Ultimate in this city.

AMHERST, MASSACHUSETTS. High school and college Ultimate central.

This is not Ultimate.

Who started Ultimate and why?

Frisbee playing was a fad in the summer of 1968 when Joel Silver, a brash, willful, intelligent, and talkative student at Columbia High School in Maplewood, New Jersey, attended an elite summer school for brash, willful, intelligent, and talkative students outside Amherst, Massachusetts. There, during study breaks, a teacher named Jared Kass tried to mellow out his high-strung students by teaching a peaceful, friendly, and fun game of team Frisbee that he promoted as the "ultimate game."

When Silver returned to classes in New Jersey later that fall, he brought the game with him. Soon a legion of students at Columbia High School began playing the new game, which they called Team Frisbee or Speed Frisbee. They devised rules and playing formats and generally had a good time.

Silver brought back the name *Ultimate* in 1970. Later, Columbia graduates propagated the game like a viral pathology, starting new teams on the collegiate level as an excuse to avoid the draft. In this way Ultimate spread across the country—and eventually—the world.

How many people play Ultimate?

Massive summer leagues like those in Ottawa, Vancouver, and Seattle

TEN IMPORTANT RULES OF THE GAME

IT HELPS TO KNOW ABOUT ULTIMATE BEFORE YOU PICK UP A DISC AND PLAY.

1. No tackling.
2. No running with the disc.
3. Yes, cleats are a good idea.
4. An organized game of catch with a Frisbee is not Ultimate.
5. Keeping track of the score is considered normal.
6. When you throw the disc and your teammate catches it in the end zone it is worth 1 point.
7. On-field disputes are settled in the following order:
   − A player acquiesces, making the right call according to the Spirit of the Game and the divine essence of truth.
   − Do-over (replay).
   − Long, bitter argument.
8. You can throw the disc into the ground or out of bounds all you want, but then no one will play with you.
9. Heckling from the sidelines is good fun.
10. Winning in style is the goal of all self-respecting players.

counted more than three thousand players each in 2009. Medium-sized leagues like Madison, Philadelphia, Washington, DC, and Boston have between fifteen hundred and two thousand players. All told it is wildly estimated that there are more than 800,000[1] people who play Ultimate during a given year in North America, most with college degrees and trust funds.

Ultimate players are approximately 75 percent male and 24 percent female. Unlike other sports, transgendered folks are encouraged to play.

Thirty thousand players join the primarily US-based Ultimate Players Association (UPA) yearly for a free refrigerator magnet.

Is Ultimate played with dogs?

Sometimes dog trainers throw a disc, and a dog runs and jumps majestically high in the air to retrieve it—but that's not Ultimate. Anything played with a dog and a disc is called "catch." If dogs had opposable thumbs, then they would play Ultimate and also drive their teammates to tournaments.

---

1 *According to a 2007 poll by the Sporting Goods Manufacturers Association, 824,000 people in the U.S. play Ultimate more than 25 times a year. Which is preposterous.*

Do you get to break people's noses in Ultimate and hit their bloody face until they pass out in pain? I saw it on Spike TV.

You're thinking of the Ultimate Fighting Championship. The UFC is a type of mixed martial arts fighting competition that resembles a bar fight between two muscular meth-heads with part-time jobs. When you play Ultimate, the team field disc running sport, contact with another player—especially punching him or her in the kidney repeatedly—is considered a violation.

How many countries play Ultimate? Who are the best?

Technically speaking, the best teams in the world always hail from the United States. A Canadian men's club team from Vancouver called Furious George has won the UPA National Championships three times and the World Championships twice, but that's only because Vancouver is so close to American soil.

About forty-five countries have Ultimate programs, and twenty-five of those have a number of truly competitive teams.

When will Ultimate be in the Olympics?

This is a common question. The answer is that Ultimate is too good for the Olympics.

The Olympics is crowded with hypercompetitive steroid-driven type-A athletes who would debilitate their spermatozoa to win a gold medal. The Olympics only took snowboarding because they needed TV ratings and teenage girls with pigtails. The Olympics is a sellout, desperate for commercial success and a big payday from television contracts. Ultimate is better than that. Ultimate is totally righteous.

Frankly, though, most Ultimate is boring to watch and no advertiser in their right mind would pay money to sponsor it. Ultimate is like the decathlon of modern team sports.

Ultimate has its own version of the Olympics anyway, a massive competition called the World Championships, played every four years. Ultimate is also one of the sports in the Olympics' second-tier competition, the World Games, alongside such notable international sports powerhouses as tug-of-war, korfball, and canoe polo.

Is Ultimate the only sport successfully played with mixed genders (i.e., men and women) on the same playing field?

There are others, but the answer to this question is "yes." Ultimate is the only sport in which it's clear that men and women are totally and unequivocally equal on the playing field.

HOW TO RUN A SUCCESSFUL TOURNAMENT
KEITH ASPINALL, TOURNAMENT DIRECTOR

1. Get fields. Make sure you have them secured.
2. Know your weekend, and know whether there are other tournaments in the region around the same time. You need to gauge what kind of draw you can expect. It's better having a firm limit on teams to create a good format rather than inventing a format to suit an odd number of teams.
3. Stick to the schedule. If you say games start at 10 AM and games actually start at 10 AM, that means all your setup should be ready, the essentials for the players should be available (fruit, bagels, water, schedule, et cetera), and you have given the impression you know what you're doing.
4. Throw a party. A good and/or unforgettable party goes a long way toward players remembering the good times of the tournament. An all-ages party is always better received, as is having a private venue with just Ultimate players in attendance.

Will Ultimate someday be shown on TV?

A lot of people assume that Ultimate will never be a real sport until it's televised. Well, the truth is, Ultimate was featured for three minutes in a 1992 episode of MTV Sports with host Dan Cortese.

From 2003 to 2008, niche cable network College Sports Television (CSTV) signed a contract to broadcast the UPA College Championships semifinals and finals. With a collective North American viewership average of 632 homes, the contract was ended in 2009 after CSTV was bought out by CBS College Sports.

Ultimate has also appeared on dozens of local news channels in North America on the five o'clock news for thirty to sixty seconds at a time.

How can I become an Ultimate player?

Not just anyone can play Ultimate. You should have the strength and endurance to run or jog for at least twenty minutes during a given hour. You should possess a college degree, drink imported beer, and be able to argue a foul call. You should appreciate a fine tiramisu. To be an elite-level Ultimate player, you should run 40 yards in under six seconds and have a 12-inch vertical leap or better. To be the *best* Ultimate player *ever* and completely *dominate* Tuesday night league play—simply read on.

AM I AN ULTIMATE PLAYER?

Ready for action?

Strictly speaking, there are Ultimate players and then there are frat guys who run around with their discs hanging out. How do you tell the difference? Ask yourself these questions.

WHAT KIND OF DISC DO I OWN?

Check out your disc. Is it a Frisbee? *Frisbee* is a trademarked name common enough to seem like it isn't—like *Tampax* or *Kleenex* or *Compassionate Conservative*. The name *Frisbee* is owned by Wham-O, a toy company that was purchased by a Chinese conglomerate in 2006. A Frisbee to them isn't for sports, it's a toy like a Nerf football or a yo-yo. Ultimate players are special people who don't use Frisbee-brand discs; they use ones manufactured by Discraft.

There are other less desirable non-Discraft discs: Look and see if your disc is small and wobbly with the name of a local bank stamped on it—*no good.* Does your disc have teeth marks from a dog? Is it any color other than white? Was it purchased in a sporting goods store? *Pish-posh.*

If the disc you use is an ivory white 175-gram Discraft Ultrastar with a swank illustration of the late James Brown saying, "Papa's Got a Brand New Disc!" then you're definitely an Ultimate player.

DID MY COLLEGE TEAM TRAVEL TO TOURNAMENTS?

If you played Ultimate on an intramural team in college, you may not actually qualify to be an Ultimate player. To be considered part of "*culti*mate" you have to travel.

If you traveled in college to play disc, you should be able to respond to the following jibber-jabber from a typical college player: "Didn't I guard you at Trouble in Vegas? Those fields were brutal, weren't they? Did you guys do High Tide session four this year? No? Southerns instead? I played with J-Ro and Bitemarks on that Easterns team last fall, you know them, right? I remember seeing you at the party, but I was pretty twisted on box wine."

In Ultimate everyone knows everyone else. If you are an Ultimate player, you would be able to confirm that J-Ro and Bitemarks are also notorious Franzia huffers.

HOW ATHLETIC AM I?

Ultimate is the sport for privileged geeks and those who won the equivalent of $5 in the genetic scratch-off lottery. If you got a little bit luckier with your genes, you'd be a universally liked rodeo clown. If you won the jackpot you would be Mia Hamm or Dwyane Wade and then you wouldn't play Ultimate, because that would be a stupid thing to do with all that god-given talent.

If you're a strict loser of the genetic lottery and can't run in a straight line for 40 yards, you probably wouldn't make it in Ultimate—although many try.

WHAT DO YOUR PARENTS THINK ABOUT ORGANIZED SPORTS?

If your parents were into the whole organized-sports thing or encouraged your athletic interests in the hope that one day you would earn a living at

HOW TO CATCH A BLADE IN TRAFFIC

CHASE SPARLING-BECKLEY

1. Think about the grip that you are going to catch with—some people prefer the thumb on the inside of the lip, some prefer the thumb on the outside of the disc. Either one is fine, but pick which you are most comfortable with and practice it.
2. Practice. In high school a group of friends and I would play cower—a game which involves throwing and catching blades. This game is useless for practicing anything to do with Ultimate, except for catching hard-to-catch blades.
3. Remember, behind every great catch is a really mediocre throw.

it—then they would have made you play baseball. You can be fat and lazy and make a lot of cash as a first baseman.

You can be vicious, ignorant, 120 pounds overweight, and play football for good money. You could be boring, impotent, dress conservatively, and earn millions playing golf. All of these sports are a better bet than Ultimate.

But if Mom and Dad thought organized sports were for greedy, overzealous parents who trust in Coach Righteous Anger or if they never considered that your thoroughly mediocre hand-eye coordination would allow you to become an athlete—then you've got a good chance to discover Ultimate on your own.

CAN I TOLERATE AND ACCEPT ULTIMATE'S UNREGULATED BEHAVIOR?

The independent, liberal, and tribal core of Ultimate is unique. There's rarely a tournament that goes by without someone getting naked and doing something stupid, usually involving leftover boxes from boxed wine.

For the average Ultimate player, modern amenities like showers, food, and comfortable sleeping arrangements are often abandoned. Communal living is considered chic. Ultimate is libertarian and laissez-faire, like a matriarchal Indian tribe. If this isn't something you can deal with—or you can't appreciate using Ro-Sham-Bo to settle disputes—then you're not an Ultimate player. Not yet, at least.

THE
ULTIMATE
PLAYER

A-game athlete.

Outsiders generally regard Ultimate players as decent but peculiar folks—good-natured, fair-spirited, a little bit weird. They see the fun in "Frisbee" but find it hard to believe that anyone actually goes out of their way to play it.

So who really are these Ultimate players?

While all players are nonpartisan, self-reliant, and committed to prolonging childhood indefinitely, some are more immature than others.

What makes an Ultimate player play? Most are geeky and childish and therefore prone to competing seriously in games that aren't very serious. Others just think that sports coaches are annoying.

Since no one makes any money playing Ultimate, many players are parsimonious and/or independently wealthy. Managing your work and an Ultimate career at the same time is tricky but necessary. For college students, splitting time between Ultimate parties and non-Ultimate parties is tricky but necessary.

There are roughly eight types of player: the Greenie (of Mellow and Activist varieties), the Athlete, the Permanent Grad Student, an assortment of Oddballs, the Local Oldster, the Rec Leaguer, the Engineer, and the Partier.

Like Dungeons & Dragons characters, most Ultimate players regard themselves as a mixture of types such as Athlete-Engineer, Oddball-Rec Leaguer or Drunken Half-Elf Fighter.

WHICH TYPE OF ULTIMATE PLAYER ARE YOU?

Are you studying or practicing mechanical, industrial, civil, chemical, or electrical engineering, information technology, information architecture, or information sciences?

Yes: You are the Engineer type.

Have you been to less than four tournaments in your Ultimate career?

Yes: You are considered a Rec Leaguer, although you could also be a college rookie.

Do you play Ultimate for the glory of winning, for the satisfaction of defeating your opponent, and because you're naturally good at it?

Yes: You are an Athlete.

Do you play Ultimate at least twice a week during the summer months even though you're over the age of forty?

Yes: You are a Local Oldster, even if you don't think so.

Do you sometimes ride a bike to practice, travel to more than twenty tournaments a year, and often skip the Saturday-night tournament party?

Yes: You are a Permanent Grad Student—unless you calculate a fitness quotient from riding your bike to practice, in which case you would be an Engineer.

HOW TO TELL IF YOUR CO-WORKER IS AN ULTIMATE PLAYER

MOST ULTIMATE PLAYERS BLEND IN WITH THE GENERAL POPULACE, BUT YOU CAN IDENTIFY THEM IF YOU CAN RECOGNIZE THE SIGNS:

1. Never around on weekends.
2. Well tanned in summer.
3. Morose in winter.
4. Skinned elbows and weird bruises.
5. Carries a bag with cleats to work.
6. Saves after-work bar money for weekends.
7. Sometimes eats an energy bar for lunch.
8. Offers to Ro-Sham-Bo for who gets coffee.
9. Exhibits unnecessary erudition that indicates a prep school education.
10. Isn't a total hard-ass.

Is Ultimate one of many strange, random, and passionate pursuits in your life?
Yes: You are an Oddball.

Are you in college? Do you have a soccer player's build and great tolerance for mischief? Have you hooked up with at least two members of your school's opposite-gender Ultimate team?
Yes: You are the Partier.

Do you preach the Spirit of the Game to new players?
Yes: You are the Activist Greenie.

Are you mellow?
Yes: You are the Mellow Greenie.

NICKNAMES

Half of all Ultimate players are known solely by last name or a nickname. No one knows why this is. A nickname not based on a last name can come from anywhere, and will usually stick if the person doesn't like it.

THE FORTY-TWO MOST COMMON ULTIMATE NICKNAMES

STATISTICALLY SPEAKING, YOU WILL FIND AT LEAST ONE OF THESE PLAYERS ON YOUR TEAM.

A-Game	Grasshopper	Rookie
Becky	Hentai	Scrapple
Beeker	High School	Shoes
Bitemarks	Hot Fuzz	SkeeBall
Bones	Idaho	Skippy
Bulb	J-Flava	Smart Guy
Dan-O	Johnny Credit Card	Sparkles
Dr. I	Loki	Spaz
Eazy E	KB	Squirrel
Fangs	Meat Truck	Sticky
Fish	Mojo	Virgin
Flash	The Nazz	Waffles
Flounder	Night Terror	Wiggles
Fromage	Pooch	Wookie

PLAYER TYPE:
ENGINEER

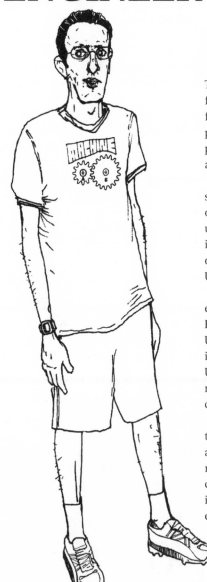

Engineer types populate Ultimate like skinny guys with tattoos populate teenage goth clubs. They're everywhere, yet no one is frightened of them. The Engineer is by far the largest category of Ultimate player. There is no team, no game of pickup and no summer league without an overgrowth of Engineers.

Since becoming an engineer is a sure-fire way for the upper threshold of the middle-class to remain the upper threshold of the middle class, it is a popular choice for college students, and college is where 90% of Ultimate players learn the game.

In many ways, Ultimate is an extension of the engineer lifestyle. An Engineer likes to figure things out and Ultimate is constantly re-inventing itself. There are few coaches in Ultimate, so Engineers can relish the role of player-coach and get to be "in charge" of something for a change.

Ultimate's Spirit of the Game is tantalizing to Engineer types. They marvel at how the game's utopian underpinnings and Cartesian principles are in a constant state of battle with Ultimate's id-driven personalities. This conundrum ensnares many Engineers for life.

TRAINING An Engineer likes to know that performing *A* will result in *B*, so most Engineers are big proponents of fitness and training. Unlike other player types who require more motivation, the Engineer takes it upon himself or herself to prepare for tournaments religiously, even if no one else does. In this way, many Engineers feel superior to their teammates.

SATURATION Engineer levels in the Ultimate gene pool are dangerously high. The Ultimate Player's Association once awarded a monetary grant to develop a mechanical device to throw a disc.

WARNING An Engineer may be a follower of Ayn Rand.

CAUTIONARY NOTE The Engineer may be cheerless.

STEREOTYPE All Asian males who play Ultimate are Engineers.

STYLE The Engineer will often wear a sports watch and must be reminded to take it off before playing. They usually wear practical apparel, like New Balance running shoes or Nike Cross-Trainers. A quality weatherproof spring jacket is a necessary accoutrement. Male Engineers have close-cropped hair.

DATING Engineers tend to prefer the company of other Engineers, fulfilling ancient Masonic rites that are not to be discussed.

RELATED PLAYER TYPE The Geek. The Geek appreciates the techniques, tactics and strategies of Ultimate. Many Geeks become entranced by Ultimate's ever-intriguing variations of rules, rules enforcement, tournament formats, styles of play and, of course, statistics. Some even go so far as to keep statistics on team play. In a fundamental way, all Engineers are also Geeks, but not all Geeks are Engineers.

DIVISIONS OF PLAY

Everyone wins.

Ultimate across North America comes in a variety of forms, primarily defined by the main governing body for Ultimate—the UPA, a non-profit player's organization similar to the USOC or NCAA. The UPA supports the Championship Series, which runs the divisions of Ultimate: **Men's** (called the **Open** division because women are allowed to play on Open teams), **Women's** and **Mixed**.

Divisions are strictly amateur—there is no money in Ultimate. If you are offered money to play Ultimate, you should turn it down or offer it to charity.

Divisions are further defined by tooth length.

HOW TO PUT ON A GOOD MARK
SEAN MCCALL

1. Shuffle your feet to cover more ground. The advantage you have as a marker is that the thrower has to hold a pivot foot and you do not. Don't give away that advantage by being flat-footed on the mark. Try to be quick and light on the balls of your feet.
2. Extend your arms. Keep your arms fully extended and low, especially on the flick side.
3. Hold your position. Don't bite on fakes to the open side. Be concerned with protecting the break side.
4. Be aggressive. The mark is no time to rest—but take a step back on high counts to avoid contact that might result in a reset of the stall count.

YOUTH (ALSO CALLED HIGH SCHOOL OR JUNIORS)

You have to be under the age of eighteen and have moderately short teeth to play Youth Ultimate. You should also attend a prep school, preferably in the Northeast or Northwest. Youth Ultimate features two divisions–**Open** and **Girls'**. There is also **Youth Club** Ultimate, which can be played Open, Girls' or Mixed. Joining Youth Club is like joining a traveling high school soccer team.

COLLEGE

College players don't often see dentists, which is unfortunate. You have five years of college eligibility for the UPA Championship Series. You can play with any school during that time, so it is recommended that you either stick around for a fifth year or transfer to a school with an easy master's program. If you play with a good college team you can make the twenty-team UPA College Championships and watch videos of yourself getting schooled on the web. College has two subdivisions–**Open** and **Women's**. The College Division is the largest division of the UPA.

CLUB

Club play is centered in cities and regions with a variety of tooth lengths. Most large cities have a multitude of teams in different divisions–**Open**, **Women's**, **Mixed**, and **Masters**. Smaller cities may have only a single traveling Open team or a lone Mixed team. The UPA Club season is in the fall; the Club Championships are held in late October in someplace warm, like Florida. You cannot play in more than one division during the series.

The Championship Series is geographically based: Teams compete in local **Sectionals** to qualify for **Regionals** and the top teams from Regionals make it to **Nationals**, also called the **UPA Club Championships**.

The **Open** and **Women's** Divisions are considered the most competitive of the four. **Mixed** (also called **Coed**) is the most diverse division with the greatest parity among teams and the widest variety of teeth. Mixed is played with a four-to-three or three-to-four ratio of men to women on the playing field. **Masters**, reserved for players who are quite long of tooth, is for those over the age of 33.

GRANDMASTERS AND DAMES

Grandmasters is a division for guys over forty who are too lazy to play competitive Masters and have tusks. **Dames** is the same for women who don't feel like joining a Mixed team or Women's team that practices. Both divisions are scarce.

LEAGUES

Ultimate leagues are everywhere. Many large cities have a **fall league, winter league, spring league**, and **summer league**.

Leagues are commonly divided into different divisions and levels of play, such as **elite, competitive, fun, hat, pickup, Mixed, Open** and **Women's**, among others. Leagues range from the very large (three-thousand-plus players) to the small and informal.

Leagues offer great exposure to the game, good competition, and a guarantee that you can go to a bar with your teammates afterward. You can also expect cookouts with kosher, 100% all-beef franks, parking lot jams, throwing clinics, and house parties with kegs of drinkable beer.

PICKUP GAMES

Like pickup soccer, pickup Ultimate games tend to be chaotic, ephemeral and close to the hippie aesthetic of yore. Anyone is welcome to join and all levels of play will be present, from the newbie to the national champion. Pickup games feature a plethora of jocks, weekend warriors, geeks, burnouts, doctors without borders and guys with knee braces. Half of all pickup players will know a good herb connection. The Local Oldster player type will always be present at pickup.

CHOOSING A SIDE: STARTING A GAME OF ULTIMATE

Flip two discs.

Since Ultimate is a friendly and fun game played in a vacuum without referees or spectators, it has come to pass that players determine all aspects of the game, including who starts on offense, which team starts on what side of the field, which team will wear dark or light colors in the match and who gets to sing the national anthem before play begins.

To decide such things, the captains usually each flip a disc in the air while a teammate calls out "same" or "different," akin to a heads-or-tails coin flip. A "different" result is one disc landing upside down and the other right-side up. The disc flip is then repeated as necessary.

There's no reason, however, that two captains can't agree to use alternative methods. In fact, two Ultimate captains can decide almost anything they want as long as they're in agreement.

Thus there are several commonly used methods in place of the disc flip. In fact, these contests are useful for just about any occasion.

1. **Ro-Sham-Bo.** Best two out of three.

2. **Pokey.** Two opponents square off with hands clasped, allowing the index finger to be pointing out. First person to poke the other wins.

3. **Vegetable-Off.** Players take turns acting out vegetables, akin to charades.

4. **Last Night's Boat Race.** Boat racing is a team drinking game and the boat is the disc.

5. **Shotgun Beer Race.** Fastest to finish wins.

6. **Thumb War.**

HOW TO GET OPEN ON THE FIELD

JIM PARINELLA

1. Keep your defender moving at all times, even if you're walking.

2. Make fake cuts only until you have the advantage—then make your real cut. Recognize that sometimes you'll have the advantage at the start of play.

3. Run hard in a straight line to where you want to go.

THE SPIRIT OF THE GAME: WHAT IS IT AND WHY?

Good game.

The Spirit of the Game, also known by the acronym *SOTG*, is Ultimate's improvement on sportsmanship. All sports have a sense of decorum and fair play, but Ultimate takes sportsmanship seriously. The Spirit of the Game rules are written down and trademarked by the UPA, the sport's primary governing body. When you violate the Spirit of the Game you are violating yourself.

Ultimate doesn't use referees because it can't afford them. Instead, like Wall Street stock traders and champion pool hustlers, Ultimate polices itself, with similar results. To do this, Ultimate uses the Spirit of the Game.

Here is the Spirit of the Game as defined in the UPA's *11th Edition Rules*, section 1, introduction, item B.

> **Spirit of the Game.** Ultimate relies upon a spirit of sportsmanship which places the responsibility for fair play on the player. Highly competitive play is encouraged, but never at the expense of mutual respect between players, adherence to the agreed upon rules of the game, or the basic joy of play. Protection of these vital elements serves to eliminate adverse conduct from the Ultimate field. Such actions as taunting of opposing players, dan-

gerous aggression, belligerent intimidation, intentional fouling, or other "win at all costs" behavior are contrary to the Spirit of the Game and must be avoided by all players.

In essence, the Spirit of the Game makes testosterone-driven type-A athletes ashamed of themselves and their pugilistic urges, allowing geeks and liberals to compete on the field without fear.

In practical matters the Spirit of the Game means that players call their own fouls and try their darndest to play fairly.

Spirit of the Game is a guideline for attainable idealism. Disputes should be resolved by *truth* and *compromise*—a foul must be admitted by the person committing it, and play should restart according to what would have happened had the foul not occurred. This often results in the famed "do-over" of Ultimate when a disputed foul call is neither upheld nor overturned—but instead replayed.

Spirit of the Game is utopian—but it's better than having your entire sport corrupted by dopers, unrepentant cheaters and beat writers.

HOW SPIRIT OF THE GAME APPLIES TO ULTIMATE

HOW DOES SPIRIT OF THE GAME ACTUALLY WORK ON THE PLAYING FIELD? HERE ARE A FEW THINGS YOU SHOULD KNOW.

1. You can't call that total jerk on the other team a total jerk, because that's not cool.
2. Being cool is super important.
3. You can spike the disc after a score as a display of excitement, power, and success, but you can't spike the disc toward another player like you're somebody special.
4. Fouling a player intentionally on the mark to prevent a huck is mildly acceptable, but fouling someone in the air as he or she tries to catch a huck is mildly unacceptable.
5. Do not get overly amped, pumped, or zooted before games. You may be mistaken for a Spirit of the Game violator.
6. If you have problems at home, if you have problems with your head, or if you've ever lifted weights—you are not allowed to play Ultimate. Only well-adjusted men and women can play Ultimate.
7. When playing Ultimate you must be free of prejudices based on gender, race, or creed. Judging a person's integrity, character, and intelligence based on skill level is ok, however.
8. You can't score well in Spirit Rankings if your team plays fairly and with excellent sportsmanship but fails to smile and say nice things after the game.

THE FRIENDLY GAME: SPIRIT AND YOU

Spirit of the Game means more than just calling your own foul. Within such a tight-knit community like Ultimate, it's important to be kind and considerate to your opponents, win or lose.

Teams should be good-natured, friendly, and welcoming to strangers. Good spirit means acting agreeably during disputes, settling amicably, and even siding with the opposition. Good spirit sometimes means admitting you're wrong. Because this is so difficult for the callow and self-important, politicians should not play Ultimate.

Due to its self-righteous liberal core, good spirit can sometimes be contradictory and high-minded. You can play fairly—but if you're sullen about it, the altruistic Spirit police will harangue you.

OBSERVERS OR REFEREES?

Over time it became evident that Ultimate couldn't rely solely on the Spirit of the Game to resolve disputes. Thus the Observer system of refereeing Ultimate was born in the late 1990s. You can't call them "referees," though, because Ultimate doesn't dig that.

Observers are like referees: They watch the game in progress, keep track of time, and make rulings on infractions. However, most observers are not bald like basketball referees. Observers are reactive—players make all foul calls and resolve disputes themselves. If calls cannot be resolved, the observer will then make a final determination.

Currently, observers are used in the UPA College Championship Series. Experiments with more active observers and different sets of rules in the

OBSERVERS VERSUS REFEREES

- A referee is the sole arbiter of rules. He or she can make a foul call at any time. An observer relies on the players to make calls and can only make rulings after players fail to resolve a dispute themselves.
- A referee usually wears black-and-white stripes like a zebra. An observer sticks to colors uncommon in elite Ultimate: bright orange and lime green.
- A referee uses a whistle to signal fouls. Observers patiently wait and speak softly when a foul is disputed.
- Referees in pro basketball and pro football can use instant replay video to correctly determine a call. An observer can look at a person's digital snapshot or camcorder on the sideline to determine a call.
- Referees get paid. Observers get T-shirts, plane tickets (if they're lucky) and free sunscreen.

Club Division is ongoing. In general, Ultimate is too libertarian, too proud, and too poor to accept the full and modern version of referees.

THE DO-OVER

How often have you been annoyed by bad referee calls in a sporting match? Pretty often I bet. Wouldn't it be nice—given the lack of instant video replay—if teams could decide that a foul call was *impossible* to determine one way or another? Wouldn't that be pure and truthful—an acknowledgment that the world we live in is *not* black and white but full of multitudinous shades of truth like a gray winter sky over East Chicago? Yes, it would.

Thus Ultimate has the "do-over." The do-over is sometimes called "return to thrower" or "send it back" when contested foul calls are on pass receptions. A do-over begins with a foul call or violation. If both players agree to the initial call, then play resumes and there is no do-over. If the call is disputed, or "contested," then, in an amazing act that bends the rules of time and space, the disc is returned from whence it came and the game restarts as if the disputed play *never happened.*

The do-over harks back to wiffle ball when there was no such thing as a "strike looking." The do-over is Ultimate's single greatest contribution to the pantheon of American sports.

ULTIMATE VERSUS OTHER SPORTS

How does Ultimate's unique Spirit of the Game call-your-own-foul officiating stack up against other team sports?

In **soccer** and **basketball**, an overabundant amount of drama is encouraged and expected. Body-flinging theatrics that make it look like you are gravely hurt after a heinous foul are often rewarded by referees. Prima donna tactics in Ultimate, however, would be in poor form.

In **football**, any sort of competitive advantage is good for you and your team. Steroids. Methamphetamines. Belligerent taunting of the opposition. Do it. Kill. Kill the other team. Football is war, and you are expected to use any means necessary to win. Ultimate is civil disobedience. You are expected to use your god-given talents, superior intellect, and adherence to truth and justice to win.

In **ice hockey**, **field hockey**, and **lacrosse**, crushing a player's rib cage with a flying forearm is part of the game and may benefit your team. Doing so in Ultimate will get you kicked out of the game.

The closest sports to Ultimate are **dodgeball**, **American Gladiators** and **marbles**.

PLAYER TYPE: ATHLETE

An Athlete is a *Sportscenter* addict who knows the current status of all seasonal TV sports—pro football, NBA basketball, Major League Baseball, and, for the Canadians, NHL hockey. Owing to the Athlete's need to be the alpha Ultimate player in any group setting, it is tacitly accepted by all Ultimate players that the TV may be flipped to ESPN at any given moment to check sports scores.

Athletes can come from different jock backgrounds. Many are crossover soccer players. Some played field hockey, baseball, tetherball, jai-alai, lawn darts, et cetera. But almost all—while being quality athletes in high school—discovered that they weren't good enough to play Division I in college and so decided to play ultimate instead. The trade-off is acceptable. While the competition is lesser and the chance to earn a living is nullified, the Athlete gets to be the ruling king or queen on the playing field.

Ask any Ultimate jocks why they play and they'll tell you it's all about the *glory.*

THE ATHLETE

For the Athlete there's nothing better than getting amped up to school some chump team composed of Geeks, Engineers, and Rec Leaguers.

DEXTERITY High.

SPIRIT OF THE GAME Low.

BODY TYPE Athletes tend to look like soccer players: Thin, fit, strong calves, six-pack abs, et cetera.

STYLE Athletes will wear Patagonia, Marmot, or EMS at night or when the weather is bad. Athletes will never wear tie-dye or lavender, unless this is the team color and they know for certain that their team will crush the competition.

PARTY LEVEL Athletes are often Partiers as well, a near-perfect combination that allows the Athlete-Partier to win Ultimate games during the day and dominate the pool table at night. However, others are Athlete-Engineer teetotalers in bed by 11:30 PM to be fresh for the game the next day.

LOYALTY The common Athlete has very little team loyalty. Once out of college, the Athlete will seek superior teams and more playing time, changing allegiances at will.

DATING An Athlete will usually marry another Athlete but may date other types for fun and sport.

RELATED PLAYER TYPE The Burner Jock. Known for playing high to stabilize mood swings and get "in the zone." The Burner Jock doesn't need to mellow with herbage: it's used to get amped. Burner Jocks aren't burnouts; they tend to be aggressive type-A personalities who discovered that a little 'juana can disguise their traits, allowing them to fit in with the game's spirited vibe.

Ultimate players from the southern United States are stereotyped as Burner Jocks. Southern players, in general, find that Ultimate meets the need for individualism and self-determination that was left behind by the Confederacy.

HISTORY OF THE GAME: A TIMELINE

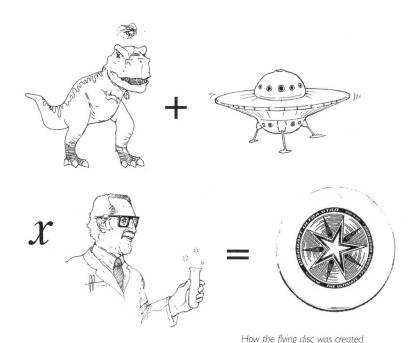

How the flying disc was created.

65,500,000 BC:
Dinosaurs and most plant life die in mass extinction, slowly rot away, and turn into a gooey plasma called "oil."

708 BC: The Greeks enter into the Olympics a flying discus carved from rock in order to show off masculine biceps.

800: Native tribes in present-day Australia make a wooden hunting boomerang to knock monkeys out of trees, which has nothing to do with flying discs.

1920s: Scientists discover that oil can be used to create a malleable form of polymerized plastic, which they use to manufacture the first toothbrush.

SPRING 1947:
Two aviation geeks from Southern California, Warren Franscioni and Fred Morrison, invent a novelty flying disc toy called the Whirlo-Way, which they cast in polymerized plastic. They expect the toy will make them rich.

JULY 8, 1947:
> A mysterious flying saucer is reported to have crashed in Roswell, New Mexico, convincing many in the American public that mysterious flying saucers are cool.

SUMMER 1947:
> Franscioni and Morrison rename their novelty flying disc the Flyin'–Saucer to sell more toys and make them rich.

EARLY 1950s:
> The Roswell incident is covered up by the government. Franscioni and Morrison end their partnership. It becomes clear that the Roswell incident was definitely a space alien.

1953:
> Scientists develop flubber. Scientists also develop polyethylene plastic, a new, softer, and more catchable plastic.

1954-55:
> Morrison recasts the novelty flying toy in polyethylene plastic and renames it the Pluto Platter. He then convinces fledgling toy company Wham-O to sell the Pluto Platter.

1957-58:
> Wham-O sells close to 100 million plastic hula hoops; steals the common usage of the word *Frisbie* by trade marking the word *Frisbee*; renames the Pluto Platter a Frisbee and releases it to the public.

1959:
> Bazillions of Frisbees are sold in the great North American Frisbee rush of '59. Morrison is rich.

EARLY TO MID-1960s:
> Americans are peaceful, bored, and easily entertained by playing catch with a Frisbee.

LATE 1960s:
> America goes apeshit. Vietnam War kills innocence. Kennedys die. MLK Jr murdered. Hippies drop acid, burn bras, protest the war, make free love, and stop going to college football games.

SUMMER 1968:
> Oblivious to all this, future Hollywood megaproducer Joel Silver learns a spirited game of team Frisbee at a summer school for smart kids in western Massachusetts.

FALL 1968: Silver returns to Columbia High School in New Jersey. He proposes to the student government that "a committee be formed to investigate the possibility of introducing Frisbee into the high school curriculum." The proposal passes. The student government challenges the Newspaper Club to a Frisbee match later that year.

EARLY 1969:
> NASA fakes man landing on the moon. Frisbee matches at CHS are played regularly by various geeks, nerds, outsiders, and free-spirited jocks in an asphalt parking lot. Silver, Buzzy Hellring and Jonny Hines become leaders and innovators of the game.

JANUARY 1970:
> Originally deemed Speed Frisbee, Silver renames the game Ultimate Frisbee and has the rules made into a nifty promotional flyer that makes "Ultimate Frisbee" look like an authentic sport.

EARLY 1970S:
> Columbia High graduates take the nifty flyer to colleges on the East Coast.

NOVEMBER 6, 1972:
> Rutgers hosts Princeton in the first intercollegiate Ultimate game exactly 103 years after the first intercollegiate football game (held, incidentally, between the two schools at the same site.) Rutgers defeats Princeton, 29–27. The game is refereed, watched by thousands of spectators, and covered by a television news channel. Players believe a professional Ultimate league with paid athletes is just around the corner.

1974-6:
> The World Championships of Frisbee are held in the Rose Bowl in Pasadena, California, attracting close to twenty-thousand spectators each year. Most come to watch the dogs and freestylers.

1975-7:
> Wham-O includes the rules of Ultimate with the sale of every Frisbee.

1977:
> The first East-West Championship is played between Easterns champ Penn State and Westerns champ Santa Barbara Condors. Santa Barbara wins 32-14.

DECEMBER 1979:
> The Ultimate Players Association (UPA) is formed by Condors founder Tom Kennedy. He becomes UPA member number one.

1981-4:
> The UPA starts a Women's Division and an Open College Division. Dozens of teams from across the country compete.

1985:
> Joel Silver makes *Weird Science* and *Brewster's Millions*.

1986:
> Twelve open teams make it to the National Championships in San Diego, California. The winning team, Chicago's Windy City, receives a nice glass trophy from the UPA, which they promptly and purposely spike to the ground, shattering it and the image that geeks can't be dicks, too.

1988:
> The UPA votes for an official Ultimate disc. On a majority tally of 8-7, Discraft defeats Wham-O. Wham-O gives up on Ultimate and concentrates on its new sport product, the Slip 'n' Slide.

1990-3:
> Cuervo Tequila sponsors a series of Ultimate tournaments. They provide prize money and free booze and introduce the 2-point line and several other rules changes with the goal for Ultimate to become a televised sport. A professional league *is* just around the corner, but in 1993 Cuervo pulls out, convinced that Ultimate is savage and unmarketable.

SUMMER 1993:
> The World Ultimate Championships in Madison, Wisconsin, feature several nude points between women's teams Women on the Verge (Seattle) and Satori (Washington, DC). Open teams Rhino Slam! (Portland, Oregon) and Ring of Fire (Raleigh-Durham, North Carolina) play naked and left-handed. Many players are convinced that a professional league is no longer just around the corner.

MID-1990S: Engineers and Geeks popularize the Internet. The online newsgroup rec.sport.disc becomes a phenomenon among disc players. Joel Silver produces *Demolition Man* and *Predator 2*.

1997: The Callahan rules for college are founded. Referees (called observers) act as arbiters for calls and violations on the field. Ultimate purists threaten a lawsuit.

1998: Coed, later called Mixed, becomes a division at Nationals. Men and women are forced to throw to each other on the field for the first time.

2001: Ultimate becomes an official sport at the World Games. Team Canada defeats Team USA for the gold-plated medal in Akita, Japan.

2002: The UPA's operating budget hits $1 million, which can buy an awful lot of paint to line fields.

2003: Joel Silver produces *Cradle 2 the Grave*. CSTV begins airing the UPA College Championships.

2005: There are over six hundred collegiate Ultimate teams in North America, all of them disrespected by their school's recreational sports administration.

2009: A team from the southern United States (Chain Lightning, from Atlanta) wins a major UPA tournament for the first time ever without their dogs on the sideline.

2011: The Ultimate Player's Association is bought out for $10,200 and 950 kegs of Stella Artois by the Belgium-based multinational beverage manufacturer Anheuser-Busch InBev.

SUMMER, 2014:
Team Peru team defeats Team USA at the World Games in Bogotá, Colombia. Afterwards, the UPA AB-InBev decides to allow professional athletes to play for Team USA, forming the Ultimate Dream Team.

MARCH, 2018:
Ultimate observers are paid. Joel Silver produces the adult film *The Ho Trix*.

2020: UPA AB-InBev's operating budget operating budget exceeds $100 million, which goes entirely to the purchase of cones, paint to line fields and a 10-foot tall glass bong handcrafted by the 2018 Peruvian team.

AUGUST, 2030:
Shunned again by the Olympics, Ultimate starts its own Olympics, called Nationals.

2040: The Professional Ultimate League is founded. Players are paid $74.50 a game and compete at high school field sites across New England.

2041: The Professional Ultimate League folds. The WNBA restarts, then folds two weeks later.

STYLE MATTERS: LOOK GOOD WHEN YOU SCORE

Just say no.

tyle is *always* important in Ultimate, on the field and off. Creativity, uniqueness, and practicality are the main guiding points for fashion choices. How do you want to feel about yourself on the field? You probably want to feel confident, clever, and ready to sky someone. The right clothing choices can help.

How do you want others to see you? Do you want them to see you as a pro or an amateur? Would you like to be known as a crafty player or an athletic one? For example, an Engineer can add a touch of pizzazz to practical apparel by accessorizing with a striped headband or yellow sports watch, possibly signifying intelligence and talent.

Creativity in Ultimate is prized. Outfitting your entire team in Santa shorts—crushed red velvet with fuzzy white trim—has been done. The only danger is in not going far enough.

That said, there's a right way to be stylish and a wrong way. You want to look like you belong in the anything-goes, counterculture world of Team Frisbee. Consult the following to craft your Ultimate style.

The 'stache can rock the college scene.

STYLE FOR GUYS

1. The **short-trim mohawk** is always *in*, while the **faux hawk** is *out*. A self-respecting Ultimate player does not sweat a nine-to-five job that wouldn't accept a real mohawk.

2. A **mustache** is cool if you're in college when most kids don't sport the 'stache. Wearing a mustache and playing Ultimate after college must be done ironically or not at all. Ultimate is neither hockey nor *Magnum P.I.*

3. Mullets are **encouraged**, usually as a joke.

4. Gold or orange cleats are **in** but only if you are **fast**.

5. Wearing a skirt on the field if you're a guy is **out** unless you're really good.

6. **Knee-high socks** are not really that cool, unless the socks are of different colors and you're tall. Even then—dicey.

7. Despite the hipster appeal of **Kurt Rambis**, Rec Specs are *out*.

8. The full **Jewfro** is *in*, but a **Half-fro** is *out*.

9. Allen Iverson-style braided hair and UnderArmour **elbow warmers** are *in* although it's not necessary to sport both at the same time like A.I.

Note: Teams are allowed only one Under Armour elbow-warmer wearer per game.

Power pigtails.

STYLE FOR GIRLS

1. **Power pigtails** can be *hot* and the **Princess Leia** look is always *in* if you can pull it off.

2. Wearing shiny **spandex** is definitely *out*. Non-shiny spandex leggings and long-sleeves are acceptable if your team uniform is worn over and it's cold out.

3. Knee-high socks are *not dope*, but **long shorts** that drop past the knee are.

4. A **backwards baseball** cap means you have good throws but that you're not always a fun person.

5. Dirt on your clothes is *hot* but try to resist wearing old T-shirts with **grass stains**.

6. **Face painting** is *out* unless it's one of *those* tournaments.

7. The faux hawk is **perfectly** *acceptable* and even encouraged in certain circles.

8. **Braiding** your hair, using **barrettes**, and **dying** your hair can all *work* if you're playing college or high school Ultimate. Such styles are usually ignored on the club circuit.

9. Any style used by **guys** is clear to poach.

Stylin'.

STYLE FOR EVERYONE

1. Backward **mesh trucker hats** are *in* because they're useful. Just don't overdo it by keeping the hat on after the game or wearing the hat sideways, which is way too frat.

2. Playing with **gloves on** is *out* and only barely acceptable if it's below freezing.

3. Wearing sunglasses on the field while playing was **never** in.

4. Bike shorts? **No.**

5. **Bandannas**? Too hippie-ish to be taken seriously.

6. Ultimate **tattoos** may be *in*, but remember, Ultimate is a game, not a prison sentence.

7. *Don't* **tuck your shirt** into your shorts, unless your shorts are pulled up to your natural waist and you want to look like a doofus on purpose, which is perfectly acceptable.

8. **Rec Specs**, cotton **drawstring** sweatpants, and **cutoff T-shirts** are *so far out,* they might be in *(see illustration, p. 31).*

THE ULTIMATE IRONY:
A CONTRADICTION IN CLOTHING

There is a complex relationship between looking good and playing well. Proper, well-crafted athletic style on the field can indicate talent, while looking like a chump probably reflects chumpiness. But sometimes the athletic-looking player turfs his throws and the gal with the bandanna and knee brace skys you. It's not uncommon for a player to look like a chump just to mock you for typecasting.

Irony is a classic theme running through many great works of literature and most of the sweetest Ultimate attire. Under Armour compression shorts? Pro-quality Nike TD cleats? They are both ironic when Ultimate players wear them because they are made for other, more legitimate sports. Irony in Ultimate is always *in*. Here are some formulas to guide you in achieving irony in your Ultimate style. You don't want to get caught off guard.

ATHLETIC MALE PLAYER + UNDER ARMOUR SHORTS + HOT PINK JERSEY	= IRONY
PARTY GIRL + FULL SPANDEX SUIT + NATIONALS JERSEY WORN OVER	= IRONY
STAR HANDLER + COTTON SUNDRESS	= IRONY
CHUBBY CUTTER + GAIA SKIRT + MATCHING WRISTBANDS	= UNINTENTIONAL IRONY
ELITE TEAM + JERSEYS ALL HAVE THE SAME NUMBER	= HIGHLY COORDINATED IRONY
CALLAHAN WINNER + KNEE SOCKS + AFRO WIG	= SUPREME IRONY

ULTIMATE-SPECIFIC CLOTHING BRANDS

Ultimate players are needy of attention. They want to know that Ultimate is a "real sport" on par with soccer, basketball, hockey, football, synchronized swimming, et cetera. It's a team sport and it's *competitive*, they will stress, usually to no avail.

Players feel loved when they are wearing sublimated polymer mesh athletic apparel crafted *specifically* for their Ultimate team, preferably with an image of their city's skyline somewhere on the shirt. It means the sport is important enough to have its own branding.

There are several clothing companies that cater almost exclusively to the Ultimate community and are therefore always *in*: **Gaia**, **VC**, **Five Ultimate**, **Breakmark**, **Spin**, **Savage**, **Lookfly**, and others.

KNOW YOUR TRAVEL ARRANGEMENTS

This station wagon can fit five or six for a ten-hour road trip.

There are several types of Ultimate-related travel, all done on the cheap. No one covers travel expenses except for colleges that offer $2,000 a year and a twelve-passenger Econoline van.

Primarily, Ultimate players take road trips to tournaments. Be prepared to cram four to five people in a compact car with all available space occupied by clothes, cleats, sleeping bags, discs, gallon jugs of water, and snack foods. It doesn't matter if you're new to the sport or a fifteen-year veteran. The arrangements are always the same.

TRAVELING WITH YOUR COED TEAM

There is no end to the hijinks of traveling with a mixed male-and-female team. There will be two known couples on the team, one or two secret liaisons, a threesome in the works and an unlimited range of possibilities for mysterious hookups, inappropriate sexual commentary, manwhoriness and drunken fooligans.

When you choose to play coed, the entire weekend becomes one long overnight high school field trip filled with hormonal desire.

Be aware that the mating games start early. Which car should you travel in? Who will be riding with you? What are the sleeping arrangements for the team? How can you change them? Who on your team likes Dogfish Head IPA? You should try to hook up with that person. However, if you're going to be left outside of the hookup scene, you should know who to heckle.

THE COLLEGIATE ROAD TRIP

For the average college player attending five to eight tournaments a year, it's a good idea to save your money for such things as tuition, food and dental appointments that will never be made. Traveling in style will have to wait.

The classic collegiate road trip begins on Friday when your team has decided to skip classes in order to hit the road early. If the tournament is between four and six hours away, you should leave at 2 PM. If it's between eight and twelve hours away, you should leave as early as possible, say, 1:30 PM.

Your transportation will be either vans or a motley collection of cars from fellow students. A car (any make and model) will be able to take a minimum of five college players.

For lodging, you will be jammed in a Days Inn room on the second floor with between six and ten of your teammates. You will get to the motel between 10 PM and midnight. Food will be scarce, and bed spots already claimed. Gatorade and beer will be difficult to obtain. You may have to eat one of your energy bars. Prepare accordingly.

Some of your teammates will be playing cards, others watching *Sportscenter*. Some will be asleep by midnight, others up until 3 AM. The bathroom will always be occupied, only one person will remember to bring toothpaste and Ultimate players—especially after a day's play on Saturday—will smell terrible.

On occasion one of your teammates will hail from the town where the tournament is being held, and your team will be invited to stay at his or her parents' house. This means you'll get to watch a movie in the living room, eat a healthy pasta dinner, have ample room for your sleeping bag, and be reasonably assured of finding the fields in the morning. Take advantage of the good fortune because it's unlikely you'll be invited back. *See pages 40-41.*

BREAKFAST OPTIONS

When considering food options at an Ultimate tournament, consider where you are on the IHOP-Waffle House line. Naturally, tournaments in the southern United States will mean breakfast with the Waffle House, whereas those in the North are IHOP territory. If necessary, Denny's will work. Masters teams are wise enough to seek out a Bob Evans.

Many players prefer to go straight to the tournament, where the usual bounty of bagels and bananas awaits. This food is considered breakfast only because by noon it will run out.

A good Ultimate player is trained to subsist for an entire game day on tournament-provided food along with energy bars, water and peanut-butter and jelly sandwiches. Gatorade helps until it runs out, which it always does.

DINNER OPTIONS

You might think that Ultimate, with its counterculture upbringing, would eschew chain restaurants and opt for more of the mom-and-pop affair. Certainly a big pasta dinner at someone's house is ideal for a team of twenty, but it isn't usually available. Instead teams know that a chain restaurant can satisfy a large, rowdy team of hungry players.

Pick one: Applebee's, Outback Steakhouse, Olive Garden, Chili's, Lone Star Steakhouse, Ruby Tuesday, Carrabba's and the like. They're all the same. For obvious reasons, try to avoid quasi fast-food joints like Red Lobster, Quiznos or Boston Market. Buffet-style chains like Ponderosa and Bonanza are considered outdated.

Upon seating, club teams should immediately order two or three pitchers of beer, a pitcher of water for every four persons, five orders of quesadilla appetizers and an extra table for the three players who are late.

Long-standing tournaments will recommend local bar-restaurants to traveling teams. Your team should go, because there will be a TV and you can watch *Sportscenter*. You will also have an opportunity to interact with the locals, which is entertaining. Remember, your goal for the weekend is to be entertained as often as possible.

OTHER FORMS OF TRAVEL: AIRPLANES, TRAINS AND BIG GREEN BUSES

Planes

Often players take to the skies to get to far-away tournaments. If you fly to a tournament, you get to feel special and more like an adult than you actually are. Engineer types and players on Nationals-caliber teams love this option.

Flying to tournaments is great if you can afford it, but there are some things to keep in mind.

1. *Never* check in your cleats. When the airline loses your luggage, you

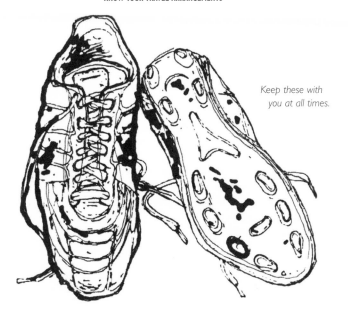

*Keep these with
you at all times.*

might not be able to play. Cleats are always carry-on items. Not playing because you checked in your cleats is considered just punishment.

2. If you're a Burner Jock, it's a good idea not to be "carrying." Try to make arrangements to score at the tournament, and use an apple as a makeshift pipe.

3. Keep a disc available to toss inside the cavernous airport terminal and at the baggage claim.

4. If you're a college player traveling by air, be prepared to sleep in the airport to recover from extensive layovers because you couldn't afford the direct flight.

Trains
No one takes a train to a tournament. This isn't Europe.

Buses
You can travel by a Big Green Bus[1] to a tournament if you really want. But generally speaking, communal living while traveling is considered gauche. Renting an RV to *part-ay* en route to a tournament is cool the first time. Doing so more than once in your Ultimate career is unjustifiable.

---

1 See page 108.

HOTELS VERSUS MOTELS VERSUS NOTELS

USE THIS HANDY CHART TO DECIDE THE BEST LODGING OPTION AT YOUR NEXT TOURNAMENT.

	HOTEL/MOTEL/NOTEL	CAMPING	SOMEONE'S HOUSE
COMFORT	Decent. Stake out a bed spot early. Pour a little water on the bed to scare teammates away.	You're not there for comfort. Get drunk and look at the stars.	Usually great, unless you show up uninvited. Works much better if it's someone's parent's house and the whole team is there.
HOOKUP POTENTIAL	Not bad, but likely to be with someone on your coed team. Think in advance about the consequences.	Pretty good. Mention how starry the stars are.	Abysmal. Siblings are off-limits.
POOL/ HOT TUB	Your team specifically chose a hotel for the hot tub. Motels are for saving money, so hang out at your friend's hotel for action.	There might be a lake. Cold, but good for skinny-dipping.	Unlikely, unless you play for Exeter Academy Ultimate.
HOT SHOWER	Yes, and a chance to stock up on mini soaps.[1]	If you're lucky they'll open up a nearby gym for showers. Bring a towel.	Yes, and a chance to sample different types of shampoo.
PARTY PROXIMITY	Is the hotel in walking distance of the party? You're set. Too far away? Stock up and party in your room![2]	It's just footsteps to the nearest bonfire.	If you're staying at a player's house and it's a college tournament, you're at the party.

	HOTEL/MOTEL/NOTEL	CAMPING	SOMEONE'S HOUSE
BREAKFAST	*If breakfast costs extra:* Skip it if there's a Dunkin Donuts on the way to the fields. *If breakfast is free:* Wear baggy warm-ups with deep pockets. A cleat bag should hold at least eight bagels. Stuff cream cheese packets in cleats. Apples go in the deep pockets. *Don't take the turnovers:* They will get messy.	Note the caloric density of beer.	*Parent's house:* Yes and lots of it. Expect scrambled eggs, Pop-Tarts, and an array of sugary cereals. Be sure to thank Mom and wash a few dishes. *Friend's house:* Nope. The false claim will be made that all breakfast items belong to housemates.
PRIVACY	None. Expect to sleep between six and sixteen to a room.	Sure, if you know where to pitch your two-person tent. If you're in a four-person tent, forget about it.	It can happen. Find the "guest room" or an unoccupied half bath. Sleeping arrangements, however, will likely be communal on the living room floor.
CLEANLINESS	Excellent. Much cleaner than your own room. Hotels come with mints. Motels come with hand sanitizer.	Bad. BYOTP.	*Parent's house:* Next to godliness. *Player's house:* Practice holding your breath and build up a tolerance to mold before entering.
COST	Start at $10 per person, per night. Add the number of doctors, lawyers, and bankers on your team. Subtract the number of college students. Multiply by the number of Engineers and Oldsters. Divide by the number of Greenies and Partiers. Add $5 if you are staying near a big city.	Usually free, but it costs money to buy a tent if you don't have one already. Double that for loss of dignity if you're forced to make out with someone just for a spot to sleep.	Free, except you'll have to pitch in a few bucks for the pasta dinner and/or beer. NOTES: 1. Mini soaps are to be saved for your next camping tournament. 2. Remember that a bathtub in a hotel or motel is best used as an extra large cooler after all the showers have been taken. The beer goes in first, and the ice from the ice machine goes in second.

HOW TO FIND ULTIMATE ON THE ROAD

Ultimate players moving to a new town or traveling for the summer can generally find a local game or team with ease. The best place to start searching is the internet.

Ultimate is well populated with information-technology geeks. Regular postings about all things Ultimate have appeared on the internet newsgroup rec.sport.disc since 1994. You should first search the RSD archives (under Google Groups) or make an inquiry post.

Equally helpful is the comprehensive list of teams, pickup games, summer leagues and tournaments located on the UPA website (www.upa.org). Look under "Where to Play." There you will find e-mail addresses, website links, and phone numbers covering all major cities in the United States, Canada, and even overseas.

If you're moving to a small town with an invisible Ultimate scene, try calling the chamber of commerce and ask what they know about "Frisbee." Asking for "Ultimate" will just confuse them.

ROUGHING IT

It takes patience and effort to find decent Ultimate action in a strange locale if you haven't made contacts ahead of time. Ultimate games are ephemeral, and players blend in with their surroundings at night.

In small cities, you have to know where to go and when. It is not advised that you blindly seek out a game on foot—but it may be necessary if you're in need of a quick fix.

Try asking about Frisbee action at the local park during the daytime or cruise the brewpub in the evening looking for people wearing Ultimate T-shirts. A good dive bar may have Ultimate clientele, or you could try to contact the local herb dealer. If desperation sinks in, call the Professional Disc Golf Association (PDGA). Disc players know other disc players. They can help you in your time of need.

PLAYER TYPE: PERMANENT GRAD STUDENT

Women of the Permanent Grad Student type are usually the reliable ones on the team. They make good handlers. They are reasonable and hold themselves accountable for their actions. Peculiarly, male Permanent Grad Students can be the opposite and make bad decisions. Like the Engineer, they can also suffer from "dropsies," a common effect of too much thinking on the field.

Regardless, both are thoroughly dedicated to the good life involving Ultimate and the great luxury that is graduate school. Working a nine-to-five job and earning a living is out of the question. The Permanent Grad Student envisions a day when she or he becomes a professor at a small liberal arts college with a top-notch Ultimate scene.

Permanent Grad Students tend to have a lot of time to spend on Ultimate due to commitment-free summers. The stipend they receive for their teaching work is just enough to pay for a season's worth of tournaments on the cheap.

On the field as in the classroom,

THE PERMANENT GRAD STUDENT

Permanent Grad Students are capable of performing great work as well as rehashing unconvincing pabulum. They can make an amazing play one minute and completely chunder a point the next.

STYLE Men usually have a beard or permanent five o'clock shadow. Women sometimes wear glasses and carry books with them to the field.

VARIETIES Law Student, Chemistry Teaching Assistant, Physics Major, Political Science Pundit, Biology Lab Technician, Dissertation Writer.

DATING At least half of all Permanent Grad Students are in the Ultimate scene to get laid.

CONSTITUTION Permanent Grad Students may have weak constitutions and can be injury-prone. Because their body type is impressively thin, they are believed to be in good shape when, in fact, they are more commonly out of shape. Permanent Grad Students suffer from ailments relating to their future profession: bad backs, sore necks, eye strain, and a deeply rooted agnosticism.

DISPOSITION Permanent Grad Students have a cheerful personality, mostly owing to the fact that they know they have a good life. They'll be the first to admit that graduate school life is chill, even with that two-hundred-page thesis hulking in the background.

RELATED PLAYER TYPE The Teacher. At some point in their late twenties or early thirties, Permanent Grad Students will finish their slow and steady studies, emerge from the cocoon, and take flight in rarefied air as a majestic **Professor**. Most will then give up Ultimate and leave the sport to younger, more obsessive Athletes and Engineers.

Some, however, will stick around to coach Ultimate in high school or help a novice college team. The Teacher can be a valuable commodity to your team and is credited with helping pass down the sport of Ultimate and its peculiar traditions from generation to generation.

TOURNAMENTS:
THE SEASONAL
SCHEDULE

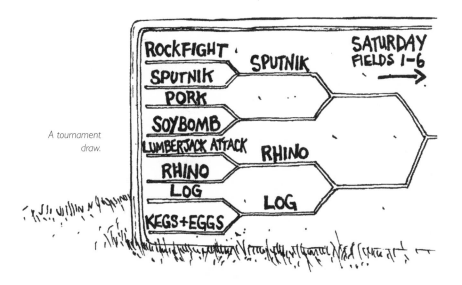

A tournament draw.

Tournaments are Ultimate's equivalent of Renaissance faires. They are part social gathering, part hookup scene and part competition. Sometimes, there are even jesters.

One or two tournaments are held every weekend across North America, more in the summer. Tournaments come in different sizes, formats, attitudes and levels of competition. All of them, however, are about the *competition*. Imagine attending a Renaissance faire and being *required* to joust.

There are two primary goals during a tournament weekend: winning the tournament and winning the party. Either victory means you go home a champion. Winning both the tournament and the party is considered the pinnacle of success for every righteous Ultimate player.

With Ultimate, it's all fun and games until one team has more fun and games than you. Never forget that.

THEMED TEAMS AND COSTUMES: AN ULTIMATE TRADITION

As befitting Ultimate's *raison d'être*—namely, being childish and having fun—dressing up a team under a theme is common. Many tournaments demand it.

Costumes and Ultimate go hand in hand like penguins at the opera. Sometmes when the line between competition and fun becomes blurred, people get concerned. Does a team dressed like smurfs deserve respect or scorn? What if they compete really well and crush your non-costumed, ultrajock team? On the other hand, what if they suck at Ultimate but share their beer with you?

With this in mind, you should not underestimate or disparage the team wearing superhero costumes. When Wonder Woman torches you deep for a goal because you thought she looked like Susan Lucci you will regret it—and *always* be aware of where Green Lantern is on the field.

Remember—players don't want to look like a fool when dressed like a fool—the point is to make others look foolish by skying them in the endzone, preferably in front of a camera with a really big lens.

The freedom to put together a team in any manner you see fit is a prized element of Ultimate culture.

THE SATURDAY-NIGHT TOURNAMENT PARTY

Ultimate is basically a traveling party circuit, so tournament directors work hard to host a good party knowing that the tournament's reputation can be staked upon it.

The party is usually on Saturday night, at either a local bar or someone's house. Barns, hotel rooms, and roller-skating rinks are acceptable alternatives. Karaoke bars are not.

Bar parties are equal parts hookup scene, dance party, and horse show. Players should prove their tribal worth as alternative athletes by competing well at the pool table, in darts, or with a bag of twigs and a piece of flint.

Houses make great party locales because there is always an abundance of long, flat surfaces for games involving cups. Houses also provide the rare opportunity to crash out on carpeted floors and cushioned sofas.

Prime destination tournaments feature camping, and the party is at the campsite. This means naked campfire games and a guarantee that the shenanigans will go on all night, or at least until you run out of things to burn. Tournaments with camping are considered first-rate.

When challenged at a party you must compete in any proposed contest—

THEMED TEAMS

IT'S NEVER EASY TO COME UP WITH A GOOD CREATIVE THEME FOR YOUR TEAM. TO MAKE IT MORE DIFFICULT, THE FOLLOWING HAVE ALREADY BEEN DONE.

FLYING DWARVES. All players are under five foot six.

DOWNTOWN BROWN. Black power! Players are dark-skinned.

MATZOH BALLS. Oy Vey! An all-Jewish team.

SAMMY DAVIS JUNIORS. Players are under five-foot-six, dark-skinned and Jewish.

DEATH STAR GAY BAR. Players dress up like effeminate Star Wars characters.

HIP HOP WIG SHOP. Sunglasses, bling and Afro wigs.

HEE HAW. Based on the 1980s variety TV show about the South; Lots of straw.

CLUE. Professor Plum hucks it to Miss Scarlet for a goal.

PROM QUEENS. Women's team decked out in prom dresses.

TEENAGE GOTH ANGST. It's all great gothic fun until you have to lay out in your corset.

GASHLY CRUMB TINIES. Deathly white face paint and fake blood stains; from the Edward Gorey graphic novel.

LAWN PARTY. Pleated skirts, collared shirts, golfing tartans, and lots of lily white.

THEMES NOT USED YET

HELLO KITTY. Big eyes, strange Japanese names and lots of plastic coin purses.

TEAM TAMMY FAYE. Streaky eyeliner, big hair and too much lipstick.

ANIMAL COLLECTIVE. Like the band; pick your favorite animal spirit.

COPS AND ROBBERS. Or S&M, your choice.

GUYS AND DOLLS. This has probably been done before.

EX-FACTOR. Everyone must have at least one ex-lover on the team

XXY. A co-ed team with short, slight men and big, beefy broads.

Q-BERT. Large cylindrical nose-like appendages are strapped to body; you may only move diagonally across the field.

BRYN MAWR RUGBY. An open/men's team.

WHITE COLLAR CRIME WAVE. Look like any character from *American Psycho*.

TWELVE TOP COMPETITIVE TOURNAMENTS

- *Winter Trophy*—Göteborg, Sweden, late January.
- *Stanford Invite*—Palo Alto, California, early March.
- *College Centex*—Austin, Texas, March.
- *Dream Cup*—Tokyo, Japan, mid-March.
- *UPA College Championships*—various sites, late May
- *Boston Invite*—Boston, Massachusetts, mid-June.
- *Emerald City Classic*—Seattle, Washington, mid-August.
- *Chicago Heavyweights*—Naperville, Illinois, early September.
- *Northwest Club Regionals*—various sites, early October.
- *UPA Club Championships*—various sites, late October.
- *World Club Ultimate Championships*—held every four years, different cities.
- *World Ultimate and Guts Championships*—held every four years, different cities.

air hockey, sink the *Bismarck,* any sort of trivia game, any sort of invented hand-eye coordination game, anything involving drinks, et cetera. All of Ultimate is a game.

DANCING

Ultimate players like to dance, and they like to dance to rap bands and funk bands. Occasionally a rock band will be acceptable. Many tournaments hire a local band to play at the party. If it were even remotely possible, every Ultimate tournament would hire George Clinton and the P-Funk All-Stars.

If George Clinton isn't available that weekend, and Fishbone, Maceo Parker, and Burning Spear are unavailable, try Gogol Bordello. The key is *energy.*

It will be acceptable for a DJ to spin James Brown, Girl Talk, Gnarls Barkley, Snoop Dogg, Notorious B.I.G., the Clash, the Roots, Bob Marley, OutKast, Beck and the like. Avoid golden oldies and classic rock.

Indie rock is death to the dance floor. Folk is murder. Poppy teenage mod-rock bands from the UK like Arctic Monkeys, Franz Ferdinand and M.I.A. are good. Almost any radio hit from the '80s, '90s, or '00s is cool. Jam bands like Phish or Dave Matthews may be awesome when live, but aren't so hot off a CD.

WINNING THE PARTY

As befitting the nature of Ultimate, much value is placed on the team or group of individuals who can stay up the latest and party the longest. This is called "winning the party."

Your team is considered to have won the party when you are the last in attendance. At major party tournaments you will end up staying awake until dawn.

In general, to win the party you must have played games during the day and have games the following day. If you leave the party at any point and return, you may be disqualified. If you doze off, you're out of the running. Because camping tournaments are as close to pure hedonism as Ultimate gets, you cannot win the party at a camping tournament because there's no way to claim it.

You can claim to win an Ultimate party by:

1. Being the last two people awake when everyone else has bailed—you need two because one person has to verify the story.

2. Being the last team with at least seven people (a starting line) there.

3. Winning a Ro-Sham to determine the party winner(s).

4. Being in attendance when the party is shut down by the authorities.

5. Commandeering the DJ and/or microphone and playing "We Will Rock You" until everyone leaves.

TYPES OF TOURNAMENTS

Beach tournaments offer quick action with smaller teams on smaller fields. At a **hat** tournament, players sign up individually and are randomly assigned to teams (proverbially and sometimes in actuality by pulling names

TEN TOURNAMENTS NOT TO MISS IN YOUR LIFETIME

- *Pie de la Cuesta*—Acapulco, Mexico, mid-January.
- *Kaimana Klassik*—Waimanalo, Oahu, Hawaii in mid-February.
- *Paganello*—Rimini, Italy, Easter weekend.
- *Gender Blender*—Fergus, Ontario, early June.
- *Poultry Days*—Versailles, Ohio, early June.
- *Potlatch*—Seattle, Washington early July.
- *Wildwood*—Wildwood, New Jersey, late July.
- *Clambake*—New Brunswick, Maine, mid-September.
- *UPA Club Championships*—Sarasota, Florida, late October.
- *Worlds*—Held every two years, different cities.

QUIZ

MATCH THESE TOURNAMENTS WITH THEIR LOCATION

1. Mud Bowl
2. Huck Finn
3. No Surf
4. Discos Calientes
5. Hats Hops & Hucks
6. Chicago Heavyweights
7. Summer Solstice
8. Queen City Tune-Up
9. Flower Bowl
10. Terminus
11. Comedy of Errors
12. Mardi Gras
13. New Year's Fest
14. Ow My Knee
15. Chowdafest
16. Whitesmoke
17. Cooler by the Lake
18. Hip Hop On Pop
19. Daweena
20. Chucktown Throwdown

a. Eugene, Oregon, and Tulsa, Oklahoma
b. Naperville, Illinois
c. Chico, California
d. Philadelphia, Pennsylvania
e. Charleston, South Carolina
f. Milwaukee, Wisconsin
g. Baton Rouge, Louisiana
h. South Bend, Indiana
i. Providence, Rhode Island
j. Salt Lake City, Utah
k. Montréal, Québec
l. Atlanta, Georgia
m. St. Louis, Missouri
n. Talladega, Alabama
o. Charlotte, North Carolina
p. Vancouver, British Columbia
q. Tempe, Arizona
r. Santa Cruz, California
s. Albany, New York
t. Cleveland, Ohio

ANSWERS

1-N, 2-M, 3-T, 4-C, 5-R, 6-B, 7-A, 8-O, 9-P, 10-L, 11-K, 12-G, 13-Q, 14-S, 15-I, 16-H, 17-F, 18-D, 19-J, 20-E

SCORING

18 OR HIGHER
You are cheating.

15-17
You are a Tournament Slut (see p. 114)

10-14
You are the Local Oldste (see page 98)

6-9
You should consider cheating.

3-5:
Hints: Flower Bowl & Comedy of Errors are provincial; Whitesmoke is in a northern town with a south-ern name, and Daweena means "last snowstorm of the season" in the language of the Ute.

0-2
Quit your day job and get out of the house

HOW TO THROW COMPLETED HUCKS

GWEN AMBLER

1. Lead your cutter with touch. Create enough power to put the disc out in front of the cutter by gripping the disc tightly and snapping your wrist hard. Generate torque by twisting your torso upon release. Make sure there is enough air underneath the disc so that it will slow down enough for the receiver to catch up with it.

2. Aim for the cones. You always want the cutter to be able to meet the disc at an angle and avoid having the disc come directly over the receiver's head, so aim to have it caught in the third of the field near a sideline.

3. Throw to separation, not matchups. How fast or how high your receiver can run or jump will determine how much separation he or she needs to be considered open, but the bottom line is that he or she needs *some* separation deep before you put it up.

---

out of a hat). You can play outdoors in a **snow** tournament or **indoors** on a turf field or basketball court. A few tournaments even offer meager prize money and gold-painted tin trophies to the winners.

WINNING THE B-BRACKET

Fortunately for most Ultimate players you don't have to be the best team at a tournament to win. Many tournaments feature different divisions of play.

Often teams will be placed in brackets on Sunday according to results on Saturday. At the 70-team Poultry Days tournament, for example, all the teams are placed in balanced five-team pools on Saturday. Saturday win-loss records then determine placement for four divisions on Sunday: A-bracket, B-bracket, C-bracket, D-bracket.

Winning anything other than the A division is called winning the B-bracket, winning the beer pool, or winning the chumpionship. It is customary to receive a case of beer upon emerging victorious. B-bracket wins provide the opportunity to brag that your team went undefeated on Sunday.

GETTING BY ON VERY LITTLE SLEEP

Look focused.

Often you will be required to play Ultimate for an entire day on very little sleep and a nasty hangover. How do you pull it off without your teammates suspecting that you are going to be less effective on the field than they realize? Practice these tricks:

1. To prevent hangovers in the first place, add copious amounts of Gatorade and broccoli to the 3 AM bacchanalia.

2. Stay away from the Red Bull & Vodka at night. It's a trap.

3. When you get to the fields in the morning, put on headphones and sunglasses. You won't have to talk to anyone and can avoid eye contact.

4. Nod when spoken to and look "focused." Keep up the appearance of a warm-up routine: lots of stretches, a slow jog around the fields, unintelligible chatter directed at yourself. Your team will be impressed.

5. Stick to playing D points until you're pretty sure you won't embarrass yourself on O.

GAMES ULTIMATE PLAYERS PLAY

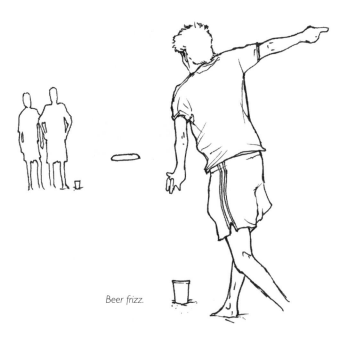

Beer frizz.

When you become an Ultimate player you've committed yourself to a lifetime of games. You will be the first to call shotgun in the parking lot. You will Ro-Sham-Bo a teammate for his or her place in the buffet line. You will play silly games, and their outcomes will seem important at the time.

Ultimate players will vigorously compete at miniature golf, bocce, croquet, card games of all types, caps, Shoot-'Em, skee ball, shuffleboard, anything on the Wii, Ghosts in the Graveyard, dodgeball, Ping-Pong, Ms. Pac-Man, the word search on the back of a place mat—the list of acceptable games is endless.

In Ultimate, competition is always on. Anything can be turned into a game: Make something up, add a bet to any endeavor, challenge your friends.

Any game learned or invented in school (like Ultimate) or summer camp is encouraged. In fact, when spending time with Ultimate players, it's often hard to know when the games begin and end. To be on the safe side, it's best to stay loose and ready to accept a teammate's challenge to chug ten ounces of pickle brine or cite five flavors of Fla-Vor-Ice.

All of Ultimate is about having fun. If suddenly Ultimate players had real responsibilities then childhood would be over and the games would end. No one wants that.

DISC GAMES

All you need is a disc and another person to enjoy these games. As in anything, the more people that play, the better.

Cower

Two teams stand in a line facing each other about 30 yards apart. One player throws a sky-high blade, and a player on the other team attempts to catch it. Don't forget to catch one-handed—a rule that dates back to 1970. If you drop the disc, your team will have to cower to the ground, unable to move while the other side gets a free blade shot at you.

Milk

Originated with a plastic milk jug when players formed a circle and bounced the jug to the ground and attempted to catch it by the handle. In the ultimate world, a disc is substituted for the milk jug. The disc usually gets destroyed.

Hot Box

Another game borrowed from childhood. Played two-on-two or three-on-three. A small square demarcated by cones or shoes forms the box. The object is to catch the disc inside the box. You have to reset about 20 yards outside the box before attempting to score. First person who cries has to go home.

500

You know the deal: Throw something in the air (in this case, a disc) and whoever comes down with it gets 100 points. The game is played to 500 points. There are no fouls. The game ends when someone gets injured.

Disc Golf

It's like ball golf, but with a disc and metal baskets that catch the disc. Ultimate players turn to disc golf only after they've retired. Playing impromptu "disc golf" using trees and street signs as targets is allowable for Ultimate players.

HOW TO SKY A TALLER PLAYER
DOMINIQUE FONTENETTE

1. Position yourself between your opponent and where you predict you will catch the disc.

2. Box your opponent out and make her or him have to jump completely over you (violation) or through you (foul) in order to have a play on the disc.

3. Time your approach so that you are making a running jump to catch the disc at your maximum vertical reach.

4. Mentally, never think negative thoughts about getting skyed. To consider failure is enough to give your opponent the advantage.

Lawn Chair MTA

MTA is an acronym for Maximum Time Aloft, which is a discipline of the World Overall Championships where you have to throw a disc in the air, run after it, and then catch it one-handed. In this case you have to run with a lawn chair and catch it while sitting.

Double Disc Court

A two-on-two competition that involves trying to get discs in and out of a small area of the field. Taiwan has a team. If you play DDC competently, you should challenge other teams for their lunch money.

Guts

Two teams of five players apiece throw the disc as hard and fast at they can at their opponents. Catches have to be one-handed. Guts has been around since the 1950s and used to be more popular than Ultimate in the 1970s.

Flutter Guts

A less painful version of Guts and more common among Ultimate players. Players on two teams stand about 10 feet apart and take turns throwing light, wobbly passes at each other. You must catch with one hand without using any other part of the body to cradle the disc. Points are scored when a team fails to make a catch. Heckling, playing "defense," and any sort of silliness is generally encouraged.

Goaltimate

An Ultimate-like spin-off game, except you score by completing a pass through a giant half-circle portico stuck in the ground.

Mini

A miniaturized game of Ultimate played on a smaller field with fewer players. You play to plus 3 or minus 2, with every turnover counting as minus 1 and every goal as plus 1. Play is make-it-take-it and continuous.

DISC AND DRINKING GAMES

Games are more fun if there's something on the line like a cup of beer. Gatorade can be substituted for beer. Boxed wine can be substituted for Gatorade.

Cups on Sticks (Suzy Sticks)

Secure two 3-foot durable plastic sticks into the ground a disc-and-a-fist-length apart with plastic cups overturned on top of them. Set up another pair directly across about 30 feet away. Two teams of two take turns throwing a disc to try to either knock the cups off the opponent's sticks (1 point per cup) or get the disc through the sticks cleanly (2 points). If you knock a cup off an opponent's stick but the cup is caught before it hits the ground, you get no points. However, it must be caught one-handed, as the other hand must be holding a beer. Game to 11.

Beer Frizz

Played on pavement or another flat, smooth surface (grass won't work). Set up two empty plastic cups upside down about 50 feet apart. Teams of two take a side, with one of the cups. Halfway between them and off to the side another cup is arranged and filled with about an inch of beer. Players take turns throwing a disc to knock over the other team's cup. If you knock the cup over, your teammate runs quickly to where the disc stops, picks it up, and throws it back at you in an attempt for you to mac (hit) it into the cup on your side for a point. In the meantime, a player from the other team runs to chug the beer and attempts to block the throw. Don't forget to refill the beer cups.

Beer Box

Same as Hot Box, except you add cans or cups of beer as the reset markers 20 yards from the box. To reset and begin play you must first take a three-second sip of beer at the marker. If you finish the beer, your opponent has to run to the cooler to get another one while your team gets a three-on-two power play. You score by catching the disc inside the box.

Classic hand-eye coordination drinking games like **Flip Cup**, **Beer Pong**, **Quarters** and **Beirut**, among others, are perennial favorites in the Ultimate community. **Shotgun** beer races are also hugely popular as is the challenging **Smoking Gun** and **Underwater Smoking Gun**.

CAMPGROUND GAMES

Pretty much anything fun you did at summer camp can be brought out to the fields to play between or after games. This is just a partial list.

Shoot 'Em

Also referred to as Shoot-Load-Shield. In a circle of competitors you have three options: to shoot (hands cocked in a gun formation at someone), shield (arms crossed over chest), or load your gun (point guns to the sky). You have to reload before you can shoot again. You can only knock opponents out by shooting them when they aren't shielding.

Eyes Up, Eyes Down

The group gathers in a circle facing one another. Everyone looks down, then, after a count, looks up into someone's eyes. If you make eye contact you are both out of the game. Can also be played in reverse.

Waa/Bunny/Viking

A player starts the game by pointing at someone in the circle. That person must then perform an action (screaming "Waa!" while making a downward chopping motion, for instance), and the person to the left and right must each perform specific actions in response. You're out if you cannot respond quickly and appropriately. Comes in a variety of formats. Never makes any sense.

More Hairy/Less Hairy, More Sexy/Less Sexy

Like Cardsharks. Usually played after a game. Teams gather in a circle and go one player to the next, guessing if the next player will have more chest hair or less chest hair (for guys) and sexier underwear or less sexy underwear (for gals).

Miniature Tanks

Players start in a circle on their hands and knees. The object of the game is to successfully crawl to the other side of the circle, over, under, or through the other competitors, while everyone chants, "Miniature tanks, miniature tanks" in droning war-like fashion. Everyone wins.

Mingle

It's like musical chairs with sexual positions. A gathering of folks, male and female. Make your move as soon as the music stops, just like at the dance club. A position is called out (missionary, up-against-the-wall, threesome, etc.) and the last person(s) to get in that position are out. Opposite-gender hookups are not necessary.

SIDELINE ANTICS

Childishness doesn't have to be reserved for games. You can practice the art of tomfoolery at any time for any reason.

Shorting (Pantsing)

The always appreciated act of pulling down someone's pants (on Ultimate sidelines, shorts) to expose their undies. Classic.

Tabletopping

Two against one. One person sneaks behind the target on hands and knees and acts as the fulcrum. The other casually sidles up and faces the victim before suddenly pushing him or her over the fulcrum, causing the person to fall backward and land on their ass. It's particularly entertaining if done in conjunction with Pantsing.

Tabletopping.
Push firmly.

MAKE UP YOUR OWN GAME

PICK AN OBJECT FROM COLUMN A, ACTION FROM COLUMN B
AND A SCORING SYSTEM FROM COLUMN C. PUT IT ALL
TOGETHER AND YOU HAVE YOUR OWN GAME. THERE ARE NO
WRONG CHOICES.

Example

"Hey Becky, I bet you can't steal that golf cart [column A] and use
it to hit on Sean Laing [column B] during his game against Smartwhore. I'll give you a back massage if you do it! [column C]."

OBJECT	ACTION	RESULTS
Beer can (empty)	Object bounces off top of sideline tent, caught by teammate. Repeat.	Dropping object is minus 2 points. Successful completion of task is 1 point.
Beer can (full)	Object hits Carly but not Jane. You only get one try.	Object remains intact, game continues. Object broken, game ends, person who broke object loses, everyone else wins.
Disc	Object must be used in karaoke routine at bar.	Completing task worth a back massage.
Bottle cap	Object passes undetected through teammate's legs.	Acknowledgment of object means game is over.
Plastic cup	Object placed unnoticed on teammate's shoulder and picture taken (known as Shrimptimate).	Successful completion of task elevates one's status on team.
Golf cart	Object must be passed from teammate to teammate, unnoticed by original owner.	Absconding with object is worth extra playing time on Sunday. Losing object results in bitterness from object's original owner.
Smoldering marsh-mallow on stick	Object must be used to approach attractive guy or girl on other team.	Deflecting object purposely into a teammate is worth 1 point.
Bread stick	Object must be used in post-game cheer.	Object used to make fun of the person on your team who takes him or herself too seriously. Success or failure should be evident.
Smart guy's visor that he doesn't know he lost yet	Object traded for another object and game restarts.	For each person object comes in contact with, bearer gets a point.

THE POKER CONNECTION

Ultimate and poker go hand in hand. Perhaps it's the Ultimate player's ego-driven free-spirit personality that meshes with professional poker. It could be the mix of cold calculation and pure one-upmanship, or maybe... Or maybe it's that both are obsessive gamers.

Whatever the reason, professional poker players Phil "The Unabomber" Laak, Phil Hellmuth, and Leif Force all played competitive Ultimate. The chances are good that a male teammate of yours probably plays online poker and does reasonably well. Even if you lose, Poker pays better than Ultimate.

Field Tackling or "Green Light."

If someone says, "Green light Seanboy," then Seanboy can be tackled at any time.

Rolling the Disc Between Someone's Legs

Also called Five Hole. Nothing fancy here, but always regarded as a skill shot in Ultimate.

FANTASY ULTIMATE

Fantasy Ultimate is based on statistics and loosely modeled on fantasy baseball. The idea is the same: While on the sidelines watching a game, you choose players for that point (or that game). You can play among any number of sideline hecklers. There are many variations of play, but a common point system is as follows:

1. For each point played on the field, you pick a positive and a negative player from each team (i.e., four picks total). You pick again after the point ends.

2. Picks cannot be duplicated by other Fantasy Ultimate players.

3. A positive pick throwing a score, catching a goal or making a D block is plus 1 point. Special plays (Callahan goal, hammer goal thrown, scoober goal thrown, the Greatest, etc) are worth more points. A negative pick who drops a disc or makes a throwing turnover is also worth 1 point. If your negative pick throws or catches a goal or makes a D block, you lose a point. Same goes if your positive pick makes a turnover.

4. If your pick calls a time-out, your score is zeroed.

5. If you leave the sideline area where the game is happening, you can retain your score, but you cannot gain or lose points while you're away.

6. You play until the end of the Ultimate game, until interest wanes or until the beer runs out.

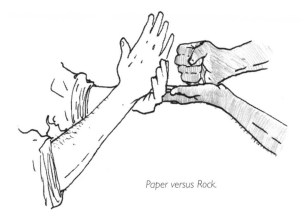

Paper versus Rock.

RO-SHAM-BO

Rock-Paper-Scissors (aka Ro-Sham-Bo) is an integral element of all things Ultimate. It's a game, it requires some amount of thought, and heckling is strongly encouraged. Ro-Sham represents the inherent nature of conflict resolution in Ultimate.

Ro-Sham is used to determine anything and everything, from which team starts with the disc to who gets to shower first at the hotel. You can Ro-Sham your teammate for his or her pride, dignity, or intensity and once it's yours, it can be bartered in other Ro-Sham contests.

Ro-Sham can win or lose games, win you a spot in the car home, and score you a free dinner. Do not ignore the power of Ro-Sham.

Ro-Sham is so ingrained in Ultimate that the UPA has posted Ultimate's version of the rules online. Check up on your knowledge at www.upa.org/juniors/roshambo/rules.html.

Ro-Sham in Ultimate has evolved over the years to include two unique and uncommon throws: Fire and Water. Both can be thrown at any time, but Fire can only be used once in a lifetime. Water is plentiful and can be used endlessly. Fire defeats all throws except Water. Water defeats Fire, but loses to all others.

Try to save your Fire to win something obscenely sweet. Throwing your Fire for the pull, for instance, is lame and while coming home with a I THREW MY FIRE AND ALL I GOT WAS THIS LOUSY T-SHIRT t-shirt is pretty cool, it's also totally worthless.

HOW TO WIN RO-SHAM-BO

If you follow these guidelines you'll emerge a winner every time.

1. Know that you are smarter and wiser than your opponent.

2. Recognize that a rock is also a fist, and analyze appropriately.

3. Stare into your opponent's eyes only when necessary.

4. Trash talk prior to Ro-Sham can work in your favor.

5. Don't think too much or too little.

OTHER VERSIONS

Over time there have evolved several variations to the traditional Rock, Paper and Scissors.

1. *Cat-Tinfoil-Microwave.* Cat eats Tinfoil, Tinfoil fries Microwave, Microwave cooks Cat.

2. *Bear-Ninja-Cowboy.* Bear mauls Ninja, Ninja deflects Cowboy's bullets, Cowboy shoots Bear.

3. *Box-Lid-Goose.* Box traps Goose, Goose eats Lid, Lid closes Box.

4. *Bacon Cheeseburger-Frosty-Baked Potato.* Bacon Cheeseburger greases up Frosty, Frosty freezes Baked Potato, Baked Potato smashes Bacon Cheeseburger.

This could be you.

5. *Drinking-Time-Nothing.* Drinking beats Time, Time beats Nothing, Nothing beats Drinking.

GAMES ULTIMATE PLAYERS DO NOT PLAY

IF A GAME IS NOT FUN AND THE RULES CAN'T BE MANIPULATED, IF IT REQUIRES EXPENSIVE EQUIPMENT OR IF THERE IS NO PROSPECT OF EMBARRASSMENT OR GLORY—THEN IT IS OF NO INTEREST TO AN ULTIMATE PLAYER.

Paddleball	Sailing	Motocross
Jacks	Bridge	Pogs
Magic cards	High school football	Non-scratch-off Lotto
Monopoly	Baccarat	Polo
World of Warcraft	Global Thermonuclear War	Keno

PLAYER TYPE:
ODDBALL

Oddballs are prized personalities in Ultimate, because they are often good players and/or good partiers and welcome in most circles. Oddballs are Ultimate's true free spirits who resist easy categorization and follow no single code of behavior. Often it's hard to figure out their source of income or their true age. Oddballs can seemingly travel the continent with ease and will often show up unexpectedly at far-flung tournaments playing with the home team.

Everything about the Oddball is a mystery that even the Oddball seems not to fully understand.

THE ODDBALL

FREQUENCY The chances of playing with an Oddball on your team are slim to very slim. When traveling to large, fun, and competitive tournaments like Potlatch, Fool's Fest, Poultry Days, or Mardi Gras, roll three eight-sided dice to determine the number of Oddballs at the tournament. For smaller tournaments, roll a single six-sided die.

SPIRIT Oddballs are likely the inspiration behind Ultimate's vaunted Spirit of the Game principles, and yet they are oblivious to their role. For most Oddballs, Ultimate and life itself are indivisible elements of the natural world.

TRIBAL STATUS Oddballs can confer a certain unorthodox wisdom and grace to a team. They can act as the team's medicine man, benevolent godmother, or good-luck talisman.

PLAYING ABILITY Many Oddballs can do things on the playing field that no one else expects—like hucking upwind for field advantage, for example. Others play quiet, reserved games until they make a preposterously wicked layout block late in the game. Some Oddballs are just good partiers.

LIKES/DISLIKES Sometimes Oddballs are true connoisseurs of discs and their flight. They may know good aerodynamics and proper trajectories for a pull. They can appreciate, more than any other type, the beautiful wax, wane, and whelm of a well-thrown huck. Oddballs may also be old-school marijuana aficionados with connections to the best stuff around. An Oddball may dislike undue obsequiousness and nosy questions.

QUOTE "How did I get here? By car."

STYLE Oddballs keep alive Ultimate's tradition of individual style. Old T-shirts, headbands, and short shorts will work just fine.

RELATED PLAYER TYPE The Backpacker. You can find Backpackers everywhere. They come in for a weekend or maybe even a week, equipped with an overstuffed hiking backpack, good road shoes, and a disc. Not owing to any overarching desire for conservation, they are nonetheless stewards of the earth, wayfarers who come and go but always cover their tracks and compete well on the field.

HOW TO PLAY ULTIMATE IN EIGHT EASY STEPS

THE COMPLETE ILLUSTRATED GUIDE

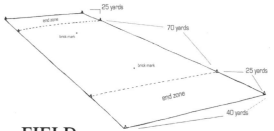

25 yards

end zone

brick mark

70 yards

brick mark

25 yards

end zone

40 yards

FIELD

Ultimate is played between two teams on a field roughly the size of a football field. Games are usually played to 13 or 15 points. Catching the disc in the end zone is 1 point.

7

PLAYERS

Ultimate is typically played 7-on-7. Most teams have anywhere from 10 to 25 on a squad.

WHAT YOU'LL NEED

These items will get you through an Ultimate tournament:

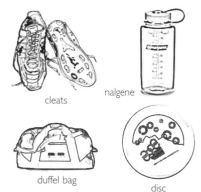

cleats

nalgene

duffel bag

disc

Ultimate players love dogs. But you can't play with them. They have animal instincts, and they cheat.

SETTING UP YOUR CUT

3

If your defender turns his/her back to the disc, you have him/her beat, even if you are cutting deep for a backhand that you will know will never come. Now you can cut back to the disc.

1

MARKING

Proper marking requires good balance. Make sure to keep your knees bent, your arms out and move your feet before you move your body. Remember you will usually be forcing the thrower in one direction.

2

FAKING

Make sure to get the marker off balance by faking your backhand and forehand, even if you won't be making the throw.

CUTTING

Good cuts are made by recognizing space on the field and turning your defender on his/her heels. It's important to time your cut within the flow of the offense.

④

⑤

THROWING

Remember to snap your wrist and drop your elbow down to throw an accurate forehand.

JUMP & CATCH

6 For optimal success in catching a disc over your head, you should always be ready to leave your feet. Jumping early is not discouraged.

CALLING A FOUL

7 If contact is made that disrupts your attempt to catch the disc, you may have to call a foul.

8

FOLLOW THE DISC

To lay out of offense, follow the trajectory of the disc with your hands leading the way. At last instant, leave your feet and dive with your eyes always on the disc.

CHEERS: HOW TO TELL THE WORLD YOU'RE WEIRD

Dinner time.

I n most mainstream sports, teammates gather in a circle with their hands in the center. They then chant a few key words of strength and unity, like "*Fight! Fight! Fight!*" or "*Wildcats on three. One! Two! Three! Wildcats!!!!*"

Since Ultimate has worked hard to be anti-mainstream, these types of cheers are rarely used. Instead there have evolved a variety of motivational methods: preposterous call-and-response cheers, tribal rain dances, African fertility chants and boorish, suggestive line dances.

For outsiders, the resulting "cheer" (either sung or screamed) is nothing if not weird.

There are two basic types of cheers: those for your team and those for the other team after the game. Post-game cheers (after winning or losing) are considered quaint but are still in vogue for summer leagues and super-fun tournaments.

TEAM CHEERS

Obnoxiousness is often a birthright of the Ultimate team cheer. Preposterous, unsettling, and downright nasty cheers are great barriers used to prevent parents and random spectators from annoying a team with their presence.

Ultimate cheers range from bawdy balladry to recitations of tiramisu recipes and everything in between. How does one compartmentalize this body of high-energy, perk-me-up compositions? There are five fundamental types of team cheers.

Posh

These cheers are short and sweet. Usually less than six words, and often just one or two, the petite cheer fires a team up before the pull or after a timeout.

"Dinner time!!"
"Stuff and score!!"
"Punch it in!!"

Sporty

Ultimate players love their lingo. What better forum to display the sport's colorful athletic terminology than a rousing chorus of "If I Had a Hammer"? Sporty cheers are those that directly reference the throws, moves, and sentiment of Ultimate.

"We're gonna huck, bid, pillage and burn, gonna huckbidpillageandburn, huckbidpillageandburn!!!"

"Lay it out, lay it out, layitoutlayitoutlayitout. If you can't layitout then do what you can—but you better come up with the disc in your hand!!"

"My mother was a handler she played in 6-inch spikes. My father was a drunken deep he hucked it to him all night. We'll sky you in the end zone! We'll lay out every play! We'll write you checks to get you sex 'cause that's the only way!!"

Scary

Some teams love to be raunchy, and nothing is off limits. Most of these types of cheers involve weird sex positions because Ultimate players are secretly repressed.

"F*ck f*ck f*ck a duck, screw a kangaroo, gangbang an orangutan. Orgy at the zoo!"

"Lick 'em high, lick 'em low, lick 'em til they nearly blow, lick 'em forward, lick 'em back, you can't resist the tongue attack!"

"Too much porn! Not enough sleep!"

Baby

In college you never know when Fred Freshman is going to invite his conservative mom, dad, grandma, and baby cousin to a tournament. To avoid the appearance of heathenism and to prevent Fred's immediate forced transfer to Eastern Texas Seminary, a team needs to have a few PG cheers in its armory. Often totally random, they can provide a nice break from the usual loud and obnoxious cheer. They also serve to disguise the true nature of the sport and confirm to outsiders that Ultimate is as bizarre as they thought.

"It's soft, it's sweet. This is the fruit that can't be beat. It's smooth, like buttah. We love it like our mother. So if you win the lotto buy lots of avocado!"

"I pick my nose with my finger. I pick my nose with my thumb. I pick my nose with my lip. I pick my nose with my tongue. Finger, thumb, lip, tongue, snot booger, mucus, yum. Eat it, Eat it, Eat It, Eat It, Eat It Up Yum!!!"

Ginger

Skanky, unpredictable, and high-energy, Ginger cheers borrow from all other kinds. These cheers do their job: They make every member of your team want to play as hard as they can right that very second.

Gimme an H!
H!
Gimme an R!
R!
Gimme a K!
K!
Gimme an A!
A!
Gimme an X!
X!
Gimme an S!
S!
What's that spell?
ARRRRRRRRRRR!

What's the longest river in the world?
De-nial!!
What keeps the dog in the yard?
De-fense!!
How do you do make babies in the woods?
Fucking in-tense!!

POST-GAME CHEERS

Post-game cheers are sometimes considered an extension of Spirit of the Game. They celebrate the joy of playing Ultimate, the camaraderie of players, and the benevolent spirit of humankind.

The effort put into making a cheer is usually inversely related to the intensity and athleticism of the game. Self-conscious high-level Club teams say "good game" in the handshake line and move on. Cheers for them are déclassé.

College squads, lower-level Club teams and league teams are more often fans of the post-game cheer.

The simplest method of constructing a good cheer is to co-opt a popular song and change the lyrics to reflect the game just played. The results range from the cheesy and uninspired to the creative and noteworthy.

FIVE STEPS TO PROVEN POST-GAME CHEERS

Step One

Pick a song that everyone can sing along to. At least one person should actually know the song by heart.

Good Examples:
"Baby Got Back," "Ring of Fire," "Take on Me," "Milkshake," songs by R. Kelly.

Bad Examples:
Led Zeppelin songs that aren't "Stairway to Heaven," anything indie rock, "Old MacDonald Had a Farm," "Row Row Row Your Boat," songs by R. Kelly.

Step Two

Change a substantial portion of the lyrics to compliment the other team on the game just played, regardless of outcome.

Good Example:[1]
Sung to "Baby Got Back."
I like big hucks and I cannot lie.
You other players can't deny.
When a disc goes up and it's flat and straight,
And that round thing's in your face,
You get *HO.*

---

[1] Credited it to the 1998 Brownian Motion team, who probably stole it from RISD.

HOW TO SHOOT GOOD ULTIMATE PICTURES

SCOBEL WIGGINS

1. Stay out of the way.
2. Shoot emotion.
3. Pull the trigger when you're in focus.

When it's right off the flow,
Cause you noticed that huck did suck, so . . .

Deep in the zone I'm standing,
The hammer I am demanding.
Oh, [name of team], I wanna run wit ya,
Won't call no pick-uh.
My sideline tried to warn me,
But that inside-out makes m-m-m-me so horny!

Bad example:
Row row row your team gently down the field . . .
merrily merrily merrily life is but a game of Ultimate!!

Step Three

Write the cheer large enough on a dry-erase board so that everyone will be able to crowd around and read it clearly. It is better if fifteen people sing a mediocre cheer loudly than if one person sings a good cheer well.

Step Four

Sing it hard and long—sing the crap out of it. Instrumental breaks must be hummed or beat-boxed. Interpretive dance, partial nudity, and a ceremonial presentation of beads are encouraged—even expected.

Step Five

Clap or rah-rah for the other team, smile cheesily and awkwardly, exchange pleasantries and return to your sideline.

HIGH SCHOOL ULTIMATE: THE SPORT FOR THE NEW PREPPIE

One day soon this player will sky you.

Once a vast, empty landscape, Ultimate is now growing exponentially in high schools across North America. This means that Ultimate will soon be as popular as tug-of-war.

With such expansion will come pop-tart movies starring well-tanned teenage Ultimate players and TV advertisers pitching Sunny Delight using Spirit of the Game. Don't be surprised when Ultimate goes mainstream.

It doesn't mean that the game will necessarily change. Ultimate players in high school will always be the whimsically athletic, just as the founders were when they started the game in high school in 1968.

HOW TO KEEP ULTIMATE UNDERGROUND

It's important that high school Ultimate players stay ahead of the mainstream or safely beneath it. If suddenly Ultimate became a tired, uninventive, predictable sport like high school football, then cool people wouldn't play it anymore. Here are some surefire ways to prevent that from happening.

1. When Ultimate has gone mainstream at your school, piss off the administration. Nothing says cool like a typewritten "Official Notice: Your club sport has been suspended. You will no longer be able to play 'Ultimate Frisbee.'"

2. Don't star in any Sunny Delight commercials.

3. Start your own team. If your school already has a coached team, start a new team outside school.

4. Keep playing Mixed Ultimate. When guys and girls play together on the same field all the gung-ho jocks walk away.

5. Rename your team "Slab Cracker."

THE NEW PREPPIE SPORT

Stereotyped as hippie, Ultimate is actually preppie.

It's strange but true—everything about the culture and mind-set of preppie breeding lends itself to Ultimate. Preparatory schools preach "a healthy mind in a healthy body" and encourage sports, even among the athletically ungifted. They teach that socialist tendencies like teamwork and sportsmanship are important tenets of life. Prep schools make everyone feel special—just like Ultimate.

New-agey high schools that combine hippie and preppie are the gold standard for producing Ultimate players. They impress upon students strong ethics, a liberal background, and the knowledge that you don't have to earn a paycheck through sports because you're probably already wealthy.

THE FIVE YEAR PLAN: CHOOSING A COLLEGE

A disc conveniently holds sixty fluid ounces.

The rule is simple: The more Ultimate you play in college, the better. Because the UPA allows five years of college eligibility, the smart high school player choosing a college will skip a pricey private school if tuition for five years is unaffordable. At a state school a fifth year of playing Ultimate is cheap and comes expected for serious players.

No matter what you choose, you should realize that playing collegiate Ultimate will make you a more well-rounded individual in life.

Most four-year colleges in the United States and Canada have some sort of Ultimate program. The question becomes: Are you interested in joining an elite team that practices frequently or are you more into partying naked? Choose your school wisely.

Some teams are party teams, some are serious, some are fun, some are geeky, and most are combinations of the above. Make sure your team is a good match because you will be spending way too much time with them.

Like UCLA in men's basketball and Bloomsburg University of Pennsylvania in Division II women's field hockey, there are schools whose Ultimate programs consistently perform well. Making the team is hard to do and requires skill and dedication. Some programs even promise scholarship money for Ultimate players. All that's missing is good kickbacks and illegal shoe deals.

SCHOOLS WHERE ULTIMATE IS ALMOST LIKE A REAL SPORT

The schools below offer top-notch competitive Ultimate programs for men and women. You can practically join the Ultimate elite just by making the team.

Carleton College In Northfield, Minnesota, a bit south of the Twin Cities. For some unknown reason almost 80 percent of the population at this small private school plays some form of Ultimate.

University of Colorado Home to the true alternative athlete in Boulder. Great grad school program for rock climbers, rich kids with varsity letters, high-class Okie jocks, and Ultimate players.

University of California – Santa Barbara (UCSB) and University of North Carolina – Wilmington (UNCW) If you are a blue-collar Burner Jock who likes to hang out at the beach, you should attend one of these coastal schools. You can earn extra playing time by fostering disdain for elite private schools like Stanford (West Coast) and Duke (East coast).

Brown University Where the elite meet to beat the East. Brown is one of those schools whose athletic programs suck, so Ultimate fills the gap. The players here are studious, liberal, and have a bizarre tradition of being in shape.

University of Oregon Known for fun, spirited, goofball teams with talent. It's not a bad idea to check out the Northwest if you're serious about Ultimate.

University of Wisconsin The Hodags men's team has always been like an old-school Taurine-filled can of Sparks: a formidable mixture of boozy idiocy and jacked-up hyperactivity.

North Carolina State A perfect combination of state school toughness, Ultimate geekiness, strong successful tradition and club boosters.

Stanford University Whichever team you join, you can be assured of a spot in semifinals at the Championships with a chance to win it all. Be forewarned: The women's team takes itself seriously—the majority are Athletes without being Partiers, which may explain why they've won more titles than any other program.

University of Texas A big state school with a large counterculture population in the heart of a city that gave us *Beavis & Butthead* and *Dazed and Confused* is an ideal counterculture for Ultimate players.

University of Michigan You wouldn't believe the number of Engineers at this school. Suffice to say both teams are loaded with them, which helps explain their success.

University of Georgia Teams get plug-and-play talent from nearby Paideia High School. Athens is a cozy and independent-minded college town.

University of Florida has always been a pocket of Ultimate activity and obscene amounts of citrus fruit.

University of Kansas Both the men's teams HorrorZontals and the women's Betty team have been around for ages, attracting odd characters from across the Great Plains.

UC San Diego Athletics here are mediocre at best. Ever heard of the UCSD Tritons? Both men's and women's Ultimate teams fill the gap and perform well nationally.

UC Davis, UC Santa Cruz, and UC Berkeley Ultimate has always thrived in California, where the ethos of the game matches the permissive weather. These three Northern California schools are equally flush with talented alterna-athletes and trade dominant years at the UPA Championships in both Open and Women's Divisions.

University of Notre Dame Perhaps N.D. is a school best known for football but Ultimate has been much more successful this past decade. The men's and women's teams are large, charitable, spirited and wear camouflage.

University of Delaware Both teams are called Sideshow. The alumni call themselves Freakshow. That should tell you something about growing up in the circus.

University of British Columbia Vancouver has lots of love for Ultimate. There's a Gaia store downtown. UBC players (men and women) regularly move up to play with the top Club teams. Vancouver summer league is massive.

Cornell University Good mix of braininess, East Coast granola spirit, old money and free time. Both men's and women's teams have been around since the early 1970s.

OTHER SCHOOLS WHERE ULTIMATE DOES NOT SUCK

Pretty much any self-respecting liberal arts school will be the type to support alternative sports. Most big state schools rock the house, too. Here are some notable schools with strong squads.

Michigan State—East Lansing, Michigan
University of Massachusetts—Amherst, Massachusetts
Swarthmore—Swarthmore, Pennsylvania
Williams—Williamstown, Massachusetts
Tufts—Somerville, Massachusetts
L.S.U.—Baton Rouge, Louisiana
Indiana University—Bloomington, Indiana
University of Illinois—Champaign-Urbana, Illinois
University of Pennsylvania—Philadelphia, Pennsylvania
University of Washington—Seattle, WA
University of Minnnesota—Twin Cities, MN
University of Iowa—Iowa City, Iowa
Wesleyan—Middeltown, Connecticut
Skidmore—Saratoga Springs, New York
University of Pittsburgh—Pittsburgh, Pennsylvania
Yale—New Haven, Connecticut
University of Virginia—Charlottesville, Virginia
North Carolina (Chapel Hill)—Chapel Hill, North Carolina
Ohio State—Columbus, Ohio
University of Tennessee—Knoxville, Tennessee
Washington University—St. Louis, Missouri
McGill University—Montréal, Québec
Queen's University—Kingston, Ontario
Mary Washington, George Washington, William & Mary—Virginia and
    Washington, D.C.
Dartmouth—Hanover, New Hampshire

A DAY IN THE LIFE
OF JOE COLLEGE

Joe College.

Waffles is a junior on the University of Tennessee Ultimate team. It's a Wednesday in mid-April, and the weather has been nice. College Ultimate is in season and a tournament is coming up this weekend.

Last night he stayed awake until 3:15 AM to win an impromptu *Gran Turismo 4* tournament on the PS2 against his teammates Jared, SkeeBall and Butler.

9:56 AM	Wake up for the 10 AM class. Decide to skip.
10:02 AM	Bowl of Frosted Mini-Wheats.
10:09 AM	Read e-mail, respond to the ones about the team and/or Ultimate. Send an email to the group list about how you beat Jared at *GT4* last night.
10:35 AM	Bowl of Frosted Mini-Wheats.
10:42 AM	Go outside for some fresh air. Seems like a nice day for a round of frolf on the quad.

10:58 AM	Think about that fifth year of Ultimate by applying to grad school. Florida has a good team—maybe it has a master's program in comparative lit?
11:14 AM	Read class notes for 1:30 PM seventeenth-century Germanic hallucinations class, then browse rec.sport.disc on the computer for fifteen minutes.
Noon	Head down hall to Jared's room to see who wants to play campus disc golf. Turns out Jared is still asleep. Clearly—not game ready.
12:25 PM	Campus disc golf starts behind Kreml Hall. It is decided that only nine rounds will be played because of your one thirty class. Lose by 2 strokes when the tee shot on 6 hits the sculpture. SkeeBall wins with a sweet approach huck around the light pole on 8.
1:35 PM	Show up sweaty for class. Georgia has a master's program in some sort of English concentration, doesn't it? Maybe that's the way to go.
2:07 PM	Receive a text message from J-Flava on the women's team. They're having a fund-raising party tomorrow night.
3:05 PM	Bowl of Frosted Mini-Wheats back at the dorm room.
3:20 PM	Watch all of the Clip of the Week videos on UltiVillage. Call J-Flava to find out who's going to be at the party tomorrow. Take shower and shave for practice. Nap.
5:00 PM	Practice starts. A bunch of underclassmen are there.
5:21 PM	Show up for practice.
5:22 PM	Jared shows up for practice. Ask him if he's late because he's been practicing *GT4*.
5:30-7:30 PM	Practice.
7:55 PM	Practice ends. Head to the commissary for pancakes with teammates. Decide that you should become more of a hucker to go along with your unstoppable deep game.
9:12 PM	Back to the dorm room. Start studying for the test next Monday because Thursday night looks busy.
9:40 PM	Study break when Jared, SkeeBall, and Billy Olli challenge you to a Flutter Guts contest in the hallway.
10:03 PM	Flutter Guts ends when fireball throw hits RA in head.

HOW TO CAPTAIN
A COLLEGE TEAM
BY DAN HEIJMEN

1. Surround yourself with a leadership core of teammates you respect and trust. No successful campaign can be launched on the shoulders of one player or captain.
2. Unify the team. Make every teammate feel part of the group. Invite them to a party, call them up to throw. The more your teammates like one another, the harder they will work together at practice.
3. Set a goal that everyone on the team can work toward: making Nationals, winning Sectionals, winning Regionals, et cetera. With focused team goals, each individual will be working for the success of the whole.
4. Lead by example. You are the captain; you are the one they want leading them. Have confidence in yourself and show your teammates how much you want to win. Believe in yourself and produce on the field. Gain the respect of your teammates and everything becomes easier and more fun.

10:07 PM	Tune in *Sportscenter* for a quick update. KB, one of this year's captains, calls to see how you feel about your role on the team. He thinks you need to stop trying to huck upwind.
10:33 PM	Bust out the Wii to stay in playing condition. Challenge Frank, a non-Ultimate-playing roommate, to Wii bowling and win by 38 pins.
11:27 PM	Drink leftover Red Bull, watch ESPN.
12:09 AM	Download old Violent Femmes MP3s through BitTorrent.
12:44 AM	Realize you've barely studied for tomorrow's classes. Settle down and read Camille Paglia.
1:10 AM	Study break: Check out the new designs for this year's shirt. Practice pivoting by throwing breakmark backhands down hallway.
1:29 AM	Check up on rec.sport.disc.
1:38 AM	Study some more, especially now that it's quiet.
2:45 AM	Finally time to sleep and think of the tournament coming up on the weekend. Dream about getting a sweet layout D block on double-game point against Arkansas and then hucking upwind for the game-winning goal.

PLAYER TYPE:
REC LEAGUER

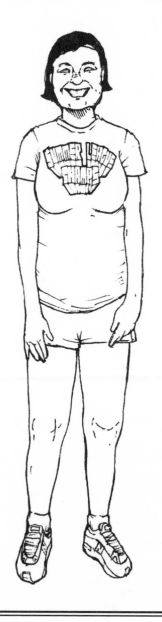

The Recreation League Player, also known as a Pickup Player, plays Ultimate for fun, a confounding state to the rest of Ultimate's self-important adherents who believe Ultimate should be taken seriously.

Rec Leaguers are Ultimate's version of beer league softball players. They enjoy the social life of the Ultimate crowd, the good parties, and the usually mellow vibe of local pickup games, summer leagues, and local tournaments.

The Rec Leaguer is one of the few character types (along with Engineer and Permanent Grad Student) where you actually know the person's real-life profession. Building contractor, nature center guide, home-care worker, grade school English teacher, accountant, and Olympic curling champion are popular Rec Leaguer professions.

Rec Leaguers are the Everyman of Ultimate. They can be found across North America and are the second most common type after the Engineer. Many full-time Ultimate addicts get hooked on the game after starting off as Rec Leaguers.

GEOGRAPHY All Rec Leaguers are local. They may not have been born and raised in the city where they play, but they tend to settle, and only play Ultimate when comfortable. They rarely travel to tournaments outside the region.

SKILL LEVEL The common Rec Leaguer from Washington DC, Ottawa, or Atlanta (any city with a large summer league) may use the infamous "barbecue backhand" and will sometimes throw a forehand incorrectly by stepping forward into the throw. A Rec Leaguer will sometimes run awkwardly and will cut to the disc either too hard or not hard enough.

STYLE Rec Leaguers will wear colors like lime green or orange when playing. Will play in either tennis shoes or cleats. They often wear T-shirts from previous summer leagues or walk-a-thons.

ATTITUDE Rec Leaguers are usually unduly cheerful, but some veteran Rec Leaguers like to think that dominating the Wednesday game means they can be playmakers in a tournament setting. This rarely holds up. Others prefer pickup games and mellow leagues to intense and stressful traveling teams and disparage high-level players.

THE HOOKUP SCENE

Girls rule.

A lot of Ultimate players like to play the field, so to speak. Much like freshman dorm mixers, coed softball leagues, and any bar with an Irish name, Ultimate is a singles scene.

Like any subculture there are common strategies for hooking up. Since Ultimate players are predominantly male, techniques are delineated by gender, and women have a clear advantage.

HOW TO SCORE AT AN ULTIMATE TOURNAMENT: GUYS

Close your eyes and count to ten. You're in fifth grade and it's time for recess. You rush outside to play kickball. You and all the other boys line up proudly to be picked. Two older kids are captains and they get to make the teams. Remember that time? Can you recall what you did to get picked early?

Now wake up and return to your present life. You're at the traditional Saturday night tournament party, the equivalent of recess. There's a line forming to make the kickball team but it's invisible and this time the women are captains.

Remember grade school—how did you make the kickball squad? Were you a good player, were you a crack-up, did you insult the teacher in front of the class? Or were you picked last?

Talent, as always, will get you places. If you are a studly player on a hot team, other guys will give you props and women will be interested. You won't even have to talk much.

Winning bar games will increase your chances. If you rule Flutter Guts in the parking lot, crush at darts or pool, or master a made-up game (it is always encouraged to introduce new games to the Ultimate scene), then the girls will pick you.

Success Formula for Guys

There are many ways to hook up at an Ultimate tournament, but the best formula is as follows:

1. Go to a tournament and pick up with a good team where you have at least one friend. Emphasize that you have no baggage (i.e., no significant other).

2. Smile a lot at the tournament party after dominating Saturday play. Everyone will think you can hold your liquor, but in truth you're soaking in glory and beaming out of pride. Chicks dig that.

3. Alpha females will almost always hook up with alpha males. Consider the playing ability of the person you are trying to score with beforehand.

4. If you can't dominate Saturday play, it works equally well to be a steady and solid player on a very good team. Make sure the prospective ladies know what awesome team you play for by asking them what team they play for.

5. Act humble even when you aren't. Women will see right through this and be impressed with your confidence. Confidence translates well to the field, and the field translates well to the cot or air mattress.

HOW TO SCORE AT AN
ULTIMATE TOURNAMENT: GALS

There are downsides to being a single Ultimate female. It can be annoying to be the object of attention of numerous players, both male and female, because single females are expected to hook up at a tournament.

On the other hand, the field is yours to play. Ultimate players are good scores for playful hookups—they are generally well behaved, educated, and free from major mental hang-ups. Of course they also tend to be immature and "between jobs": not exactly marriage material. Ultimate players are also notoriously unreliable and they rarely use dental floss.

Being female and looking for action at an Ultimate tournament is like hunting deer in a disco. Even if the metaphor doesn't make sense you can't screw it up.

The Nine Steps of a Tournament Hookup:
How to Get Your Man

How do you select, lure, and then bag a prospective evening mate at an Ultimate tournament? Forthwith is the standard nine-step process:

1. On Saturday, see how they play. Find out if your "game" has game.

2. Intoxication. This is made easier by extreme dehydration, physical exhaustion, and Pabst Blue Ribbon.

3. Scout out the prey. You'll have your chance at the team dinner or tournament party.

4. Approach target. Introduce self (if introductions have not already been made), and initiate physical contact. Already your chances of success will be good, although it is not uncommon for your selection to have several suitors if he is a good player. You may have to move on to your second choice.

5. Confirm choice by finding a dark corner, empty hammock, unoccupied bathroom, or backseat of someone's car and proceed towards mutual molestation, heavy petting, and serious making out. You are now on the same kickball team.

6. Cuddle. Sleep.

7. Wake up in strange location. Chug Nalgene of water to obviate hangover. Check the time and call your captain to find out when the game starts. Re-introduce yourself to the person sleeping next to you. Try to get his real name. Most guys will only be known by their last name or a nickname like Idaho or Kringle. They may soon be known as GFLW—Guy From Last Weekend.

8. Play your Sunday games. During your bye round, meet your hook-up to find out the basics: Where he lives, how old he is, what his occupation is,

Sometimes you may be left with a choice of the above.

and his marital status. You should also find out what tournaments he is planning on attending in the future so you can make sure to be there—or make sure to avoid. Assess possibilities for future dating.

9. Repeat as necessary.

HOW TO GET A LAYOUT D BLOCK

KATEY FORTH

1. Bait and block. Trick the thrower into thinking the cutter is open. How? By being slightly out of position.

2. Position. Be on the inside track, a little behind your person. In the stack, if you're faster than your opponent, stand just behind his or her inside shoulder facing the open side. If you're slower, face your opponent on the open side to maintain a cushion; this allows you to be within a step or two after you turn and commit.

3. Anticipate when and where the thrower will throw, so you can ignite the burners three steps in advance.

4. When you commit, you'll need a burst of energy—or gangle arms. Hit the gym for some plyos.

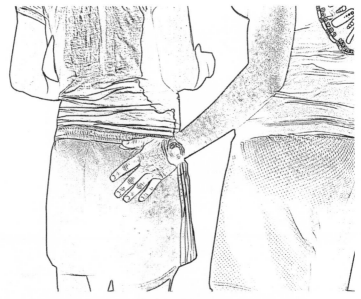

Good consolation.

HOW TO SCORE AT AN ULTIMATE TOURNAMENT: LESBIANS AND BISEXUALS

So you've got a raging player crush. Girl-girl hookups tend to be more organic than random tourney hookups, and usually occur between teammates. So the good news is, you don't have to get completely trashed to score. The bad news is, awkwardness may plague you for the remainder of the season. If you're willing to risk it, here's how to move it from the field to the bed.

1. Be proactive about getting into the same hotel room as your crush(es), and then the same bed. If you leave this to chance, you'll end up with whoever was in your car.

2. Every time your crush has the disc, cut for her. When you have the disc, throw to your crush whenever possible. Duh. When things go well, high-five, chest bump, and generally touch each other a lot. When things do not go well, pats on the butt and pats on the back are good consolation.

3. Engage in horseplay. Anything from arm wrestling at dinner to skinny-dipping in the hotel pool. Pillow fights are cliché but always fun.

4. Back in the hotel room, give your crush a massage.

5. Get cozy when the lights go off. Wait until other teammates seem to be asleep. Or not.

CAN THE FUN GO ON? DATING, LIVING TOGETHER, AND MARRIAGE

DATING

Dating an Ultimate player is not recommended unless you are also an Ultimate player. Ultimate is an attractive cult that appears to be mainstream but isn't—like Scientology, but without the cash and Hollywood connections.

If you do end up dating an Ultimate player you should have a limitless capacity for coping with child-like behavior. Ultimate players are addicted to fun and need constant competition in their lives.

When Ultimate players date each other they should acknowledge certain rules of the game. First, if they play together on the same team, they have to make every effort to catch each other's swilly throws. If they are on separate teams, they must acknowledge that team loyalties come before the relationship.

Note: Ultimate players are free to hook up with non-Ultimate players, but it won't happen at a tournament. Tournaments are strictly inbred affairs, and any interaction with the locals is considered perverse.

LIVING TOGETHER

As an Ultimate player living with another Ultimate player you will share an understanding of dirty laundry, unexplained bruises, time spent rehashing plays from the past weekend, and obsessive Ultimate scene gossip.

Ultimate friends will crash at your house when they are in town. Mysterious e-mails from members of the opposite sex will be about Ultimate.

Your relationship may be subject to frequent $2 bets on random trivia. Watching sports on television is a bonding moment, and dinner parties will be held with other Ultimate couples.

HOW TO PLAY WITH YOUR OFF HAND

MIKE GRANT

1. Don't establish a pivot foot until you're ready to throw, understanding that using opposite footwork is necessary when using your off hand.

2. Engage and isolate your core to create more power on the wrist snap. This adds tighter spin and distance to the throw.

3. Work on off-leg flexibility to maximize the lunge. Your off leg is not as naturally flexible, but it's important for getting the throw off around a mark.

MARRIAGE AND BREEDING

Marrying another Ultimate player can be rewarding. Marriage means that both players accept a life that will revolve around games with Ultimate being the primary one.

Before taking your vows you should openly acknowledge which member of the union is the better player, or at least pretend to acknowledge. This is important; otherwise the marriage is built on shaky ground.

If you decide to have kids in addition to the Labrador retriever, you should realize that they will invariably rebel against Ultimate because parents aren't supposed to do cool, weird things. You can encourage them to play sports, but you won't be able to push them in one direction or another.

Remember that arguments on the field stay on the field. You don't want to bring talk of unwise hucks from yesterday's summer-league finals into the household.

CHOOSING A NAME FOR YOUR ULTIMATE TEAM

One good thing about not getting paid is not having corporate sponsors. Ultimate teams aren't named Mighty Ducks, Raptors, or Red Bulls and they don't have to compete in paid-for state-of-the-art facilities. Instead teams get to call themselves whatever ridiculous or unfunny name they want and pay for field space.

A Hodag.

Choosing a name for your team is a deceptively complicated chore. There are many variations, and everything is acceptable. You want to call your team Burning Couch? Go for it. How about Hobo Sexual? Survey says yes. If your school teams call themselves the Pirates why not name the Ultimate team the Irates? Done and done.

Just don't name your team anything that's a sports cliché, like Wildcats, Bobcats, Mountain Lions, Jaguars, Tigers, Cougars, Panthers, etc. Ultimate doesn't do that.

TEAM NAME CATEGORIES

Here are some common categories with proven examples to help you find the name that suits your team best.

Pop-Culture Reference

Pick something cool in pop culture and steal it. Pop-culture references are universally applauded in Ultimate.

Flaming Moe, En Sabah Nur, Ring of Fire, Lick My Love Pump, Ludicrous Speed, RedFish BlueFish, Sneetches, Trigger Hippy, Johnny Chimpo, Fishheads

Pop-Culture Puns

Pick something cool in pop culture and make a pun on it. Puns relating to the game are most common.

Stack to the Future, Furious George, Huck Norris, Hyzer Soze, Violet Femmes, Karmageddon, Apes of Wrath, The Huckstables, Slow White, Princess Layout

Unique

Design your own personality. Make something up, or make it look like you did.

Bashing Piñatas, Mamabird, Bloodthirsty, Horrorzontals, Ugmo, Mr. Briefcase, Germ Circus, Pie Queens, Donkey Bomb

Risqué

Suggestion of the naughty never goes out of style. Remember that team names are gender-specific.

Sack Lunch (Open team), Box Lunch (Women's team), Seamen, Pink Posse, Lotus Eaters, Doctor Hotdog, Holes and Poles, Truck Stop Glory Hole, Flying Snatch, Triple Nipple, Money $hot, Barely Legal, Whore $hack

Arena Football

Arena football names tend to be monosyllabic and aggressive, with no reference to wild animals. They work by reminding opponents that Ultimate is a "competitive" sport and the team a serious one.

Amp, Fury, Fist, Riot, Revolver, Rival, Diablo, Ambush, Element, Storm, Wicked, Rogue, Monster, Mischief, Kali

POSSIBLE DRUG REFERENCES

WE'RE NOT SAYING THESE TEAM NAMES ARE REFERENCES TO ILLICIT DRUGS, BUT THEY PROBABLY ARE REFERENCES TO ILLICIT DRUGS.

Bombing Madd Fatties
Buds
Chronic
We Smoke Weed
Crack Babies
Stoned Clown
Joint Chiefs
Wey-Hi
Meth
Mauvaises Herbes

What team is this player on?

COLLEGE TEAM NAMES: THE ANTI-ESTABLISHMENT

The University of Wisconsin–Madison supports dozens of athletic programs regulated by the NCAA, ranging from ice hockey to golf, all bearing identical red-and-white school colors and the name Badgers. But the men's Ultimate team is called the Hodags and their colors are baby blue and white. The women's team is called Bella Donna.

Ultimate teams love to maintain their freedom and independent spirit. An Ultimate team coddled by the school administration isn't cool—but playing in a nationally televised championship under a name of dubious origin like Mamabird is.

You can choose to follow your school and keep the school name and colors, but why not make up your own? Ultimate is one of the few club sports (along with the Chess Club and Pastry Team) that regularly invents and maintains team identities completely separate from the school.

Primates

The closest animals to humans remain perpetually amusing for their child-like similarity to Ultimate players.

Furious George, Enough Monkeys, Six Trained Monkeys, Monkey Love, Monkey Knife Fight, Gorilla Foot, Blue Monkey, Brass Monkey, Spider Monkeys, Apes of Wrath, Chimpin' Ain't Easy

Non-primate Beasts

Fierce animal names are beloved by most sports teams; more benign creatures are appropriate for Ultimate.

Condors, Sockeye, Goat, Pony, Black Cat, Dogs, Houndz, Iguana, Madcow, Kodiak, Rhino, Hippo

Violence

It's a fact of life that sports teams are always doing battle. The fiercer your team sounds the better you'll play.

Revolver, Magnum, Colt .45, Gunslingers, Fatality, Berzerkers, Nemesis, Gung-Ho, Rage, Axemen

Geeky

You can choose this route if you like, but no one will tell you when it's gone too far. Options are limitless.

Dangerzone, Burning Couch, Psycaughtit, Air Squids, Ow!, Brownian Motion, Disco Bananas, Buckets, Threat Level Midnight, Torontula, Spoonheads, Haggis, Disco Inferno, Levitation Holmes

Tournament Team Names

In theory and in practice, you can have a different team and different team name for every tournament. Some tournaments expect it. At Poultry Days teams are named for anything and everything chicken.

Poultrygeist, Mighty Clucks, Party Fowl, My Chick in a Box, Ritalhens, Roosterfarians, Dixie Chickens, Hoosierchicken?, Denver Omelettes

At Wildwood, beach themes are standard fare.

Sea Sick, Swashbucklers and Sea Hags, Reefburners, Sandy Panties, No Grass for U, Big Hair Sand Fleas, Clam Diggers, Surreptitious Seamonkeys

Indie Rock

The indie rock name is usually a pop culture reference, ideally with an ironic twist or pun. It should convey creativity, verve and detached wit. Anything your friends think sounds cool but you know is cool is going to be indie rock.

INDIE ROCK OR ULTIMATE?

DECIDE IF THE FOLLOWING NAMES ARE AN INDIE ROCK BAND, AN ULTIMATE TEAM, OR BOTH.

1. Cobra Kai
2. Sweep The Leg Johnny
3. Sticky Fingers
4. Drive Thru Liquor
5. Handsome Boy Modeling School
6. Optimus Lime
7. Kill My Landlord
8. Ugly Holiday Sweaters
9. She Wants Revenge
10. Guard, Seize Them!
11. Tacks, The Boy Disaster
12. Semi Precious Weapons
13. Sparkle Motion

14. ¡The Salsa Police!
15. Professor Murder
16. Smoking Popes
17. Burning Skirts
18. Boss Hog
19. Sub Zero
20. Hella
21. Wolf Parade
22. Meddling Kids
23. Drive-By Truckers
24. Make Out Club
25. Friends With Benefits

ANSWERS

1-BOTH, 2-BAND, 3-TEAM, 4-TEAM, 5-BAND, 6-TEAM, 7-TEAM, 8-TEAM, 9-BAND, 10-TEAM, 11-BAND, 12-BAND, 13-TEAM, 14-TEAM, 15-BAND, 16-BAND, 17-TEAM, 18-BOTH, 19-BOTH, 20-BOTH, 21-BAND, 22-TEAM, 23-BAND, 24-TEAM, 25-TEAM

THE BEACH: ULTIMATE'S LITTLE SANDBOX

Face-plant.

The image of beachgoing boobs throwing barbecue backhands stymied Ultimate's appeal on sand until the mid-1990s. Ultimate players then realized that the beach is a great place to party shirtless.

Beach tournaments are the equivalent of indoor soccer for the Ultimate set. Games are played four-on-four or five-on-five on smaller fields. Endurance and speed are neutralized while quickness and throwing precision are amplified.

Sand, unlike firm ground, is easy on the body when you dive for a disc. If you are able to perfect your timing, you can lay out and land face-first.

BEACH TOUR '10

Hit the beach at these popular North American tournaments.

- *Lei-Out.* Santa Monica, California, mid-January.
- *One Love, One Beach.* San Diego, California, mid-April.
- *Texas Beach Ultimate Fest.* Galveston Texas, mid-June.
- *Chicago Sandblast.* Chicago, Illinois, early July.
- *Wildwood.* Wildwood, New Jersey, late July.
- *Parlee Beach.* Shediac, New Brunswick (near Nova Scotia), late July.
- *Ocean Beach* in San Francisco has a high-level pickup scene almost year-round.

PLAYER TYPE:
LOCAL OLDSTER

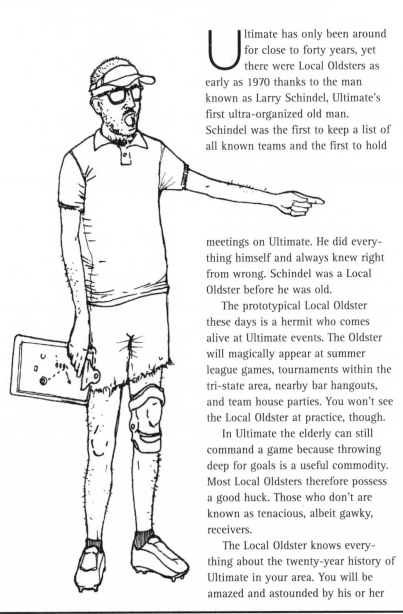

Ultimate has only been around for close to forty years, yet there were Local Oldsters as early as 1970 thanks to the man known as Larry Schindel, Ultimate's first ultra-organized old man. Schindel was the first to keep a list of all known teams and the first to hold

meetings on Ultimate. He did everything himself and always knew right from wrong. Schindel was a Local Oldster before he was old.

The prototypical Local Oldster these days is a hermit who comes alive at Ultimate events. The Oldster will magically appear at summer league games, tournaments within the tri-state area, nearby bar hangouts, and team house parties. You won't see the Local Oldster at practice, though.

In Ultimate the elderly can still command a game because throwing deep for goals is a useful commodity. Most Local Oldsters therefore possess a good huck. Those who don't are known as tenacious, albeit gawky, receivers.

The Local Oldster knows everything about the twenty-year history of Ultimate in your area. You will be amazed and astounded by his or her wealth of invaluable Ultimate advice. However, Local Oldsters are not prone to dispensing wisdom, but rather toward telling stories about themselves. They will also tell you what you're doing wrong on the field.

STORYTELLING Local Oldsters are unlimited repositories of tales from former teams, tournaments from the previous decade and players of yore. Every Local Oldster story will involve the Local Oldster himself. The stories range from elucidating to entertaining to self-aggrandizing and obtuse.

HISTORY Local Oldsters are a growing demographic, but their temperament, skills, and status are becoming increasingly marginalized by the burgeoning high school and college scenes. Will they survive? Of course.

DISPOSITION Typically surly and prone to making unnecessary foul calls.

GENDER Most Local Oldsters are male, as women start having children around this age, making their Ultimate career much more sporadic.

LOCALE Local Oldsters are usually confined to ruling their domains in small and medium-sized cities without a major university presence.

QUOTE "I know what I'm doing and I know that was a rules violation."

NEW RULES The Local Oldster will never remember the new pick rule and in all disputes will default to the 9th edition or earlier.

RELATED PLAYER TYPES The **Tournament Director** and the **Bureaucrat**. Bureaucrats and Tournament Directors are Ultimate's versions of soccer moms, baseball dads, and high school hall monitors rolled into one. The Bureaucrat is usually in his or her late twenties but, owing to a peculiar quirk in personality, behaves much like a middle-aged suburban homeowner with a 401(k) plan. Likewise, the Tournament Director can be of any age but is behaviorally akin to the Oldster.

The **Recreation Oldster**. A Local Oldster past his or her prime inhabiting the local pickup scene playing mediocre but friendly Ultimate has reverted to a Rec Leaguer and is thus known as a Recreation Oldster. For the Recreation Oldster, the summer-league social scene is prized and fresh air is critical. Seeing old friends is what Ultimate is about, as is living off stories of your past. Recreation Oldsters keep Ultimate grounded, in a good way.

PARLEZ-VOUS DISC? ULTIMATE OVERSEAS

Bring your cleats.

Pickup games and Ultimate tournaments can be found across the globe. Ultimate has spread particularly well in Europe since it began in the mid-1970s and today you can find teams in all major EU cities. Like ordering a Coca-Cola in France or rap music in Spain, Ultimate is commonly played in English.

Ultimate is also particularly popular in Australia, Colombia, Japan, New Zealand, Singapore, Venezuela and many other countries. Unlike North Americans, most international players aren't smarmy college kids. You will, however, find smarmy college kids playing Ultimate overseas who are American and Canadian students studying abroad.

GUEST LODGING

THE GENERAL RULES FOR CRASHING AT A STRANGER'S RESIDENCE OVERSEAS ARE AS FOLLOWS:

1. Bring wine or beer.
2. Be prepared to cook. An American who can cook pasta *al dente* is especially prized.
3. Proper guest etiquette is to stay for three days or less. Seven days is the maximum and considered terrible manners.
4. Offer to host your new friend at your residence back home if he or she will be traveling in the future.
5. Don't feed the monkeys.

HOW TO FIND A GAME AND A PLACE TO STAY WHEN TRAVELING ABROAD

There are two methods for finding a game of Ultimate when traveling internationally. One is to prepare in advance; the other is to go with the flow.

If you're traveling without a rigid schedule and need an Ultimate fix in a new country, you need to look around. Countries without a well-established Ultimate scene will have a single game dominated by beer-swilling free-spirit expatriates from America, England, Canada and Australia. Ask around town for "Gringos with Frisbees."

To find good competitive tournaments from just about everywhere, make sure to browse the website www.ffindr.com and its listings for hundreds of tournaments worldwide.

Preparing in advance is easier. As an Ultimate player, you are entitled to certain membership privileges. The most important of these is a free place to stay when traveling.

Your first step to free lodging is to find a "connector" before you leave— a point person with local names and/or knowledge of the country you will be visiting. The connector will be one of your Ultimate friends who has lived or traveled overseas and played Ultimate. He or she will be able to provide you with the e-mail address of a player in Jakarta or Kiev or Shanghai. E-mail your new contact; mention that you're an Ultimate player and when you'll be in town.

Chances are good that the person will help you out by offering a place to stay, suggesting a friend's flat or telling you of cheap housing options. Ultimate can be good coin.

When traveling abroad as an Ultimate player, you usually don't need to know the local language (exception: France).

THE EXPAT SCENE

THERE ARE PICKUP GAMES AND ULTIMATE TOURNAMENTS
ALL OVER THE GLOBE. CONSULT THE FOLLOWING
TO FIND IF YOUR DESTINATION HAS A LOT OF ULTIMATE
TO PLAY OR JUST A LITTLE.

HIGH LEVEL OF ACTIVITY
(MOST CITIES HAVE TRAVELING TEAMS, PICKUP IS AVAILABLE
EVEN IN SMALL TOWNS, PLAYERS DRINK GOOD BEER)

Australia, Belgium, Canada, Colombia, Denmark, France, Germany,
Japan, The Netherlands, North Carolina, Singapore, Switzerland,
Québec, United Kingdom, Venezuela

MEDIUM LEVEL OF ACTIVITY
(TEAMS AND PICKUP IN MAJOR CITIES, PLAYERS TEND TO
PREFER WINE, SPRITZERS, OR LOCAL CONCOCTIONS)

Austria (in and around Vienna), China, Czech Republic (especially
Prague), Finland (Espoo, Helsinki, Turku), Ireland (Dublin), Italy
(especially northern cities), New Zealand, Norway, Philippines (Manila,
Cebu, Boracay), Russia (St. Petersburg, Moscow), Slovakia (Bratislava),
Spain (Barcelona, Madrid, Tenerife), Sweden (Göteborg)

LOW LEVEL OF ACTIVITY
(FEW TEAMS, SCATTERED PICKUP, LOTS OF EXPATS
DRINKING CHEAP LOCAL BEER)

Argentina, Brazil, Chile, Costa Rica, Estonia, Hungary, Iceland, India,
Indonesia, Israel, Latvia, Lithuania, Luxembourg, Malaysia, Mexico,
Morocco, Peru, Poland, Portugal, South Carolina, South Africa,
South Korea, Taiwan, Thailand, Ukraine, Vietnam

WHAT KIND OF ULTIMATE TO EXPECT

Ultimate is different depending on where you're going. When traveling to
the magical northern lands of Québec, Sweden, Finland, Denmark, and
Norway, you should bring tennis shoes for playing indoor Ultimate in gyms.
When traveling to the Tenerife Islands off the coast of Spain, or Tel Aviv,
Israel, bring sun block for beach Ultimate. If you're heading to Southeast
Asia, *leave the herb behind.* Carrying marijuana in this part of the world may
get you hanged. Conversely, when traveling to Switzerland, bring an open
mind for cannabis. The most famous Swiss team is called Red I's and they
are known to make a spectacularly spacey Swiss hot cocoa.

THE ENGLISH

FORMER COLONIALISTS AND PURVEYORS OF THE COMMON TONGUE PLAY A LOT OF DISC. HERE IS A SCOUTING REPORT OF THE TYPICAL ENGLISH ULTIMATE SCENE:

1. Cool English lads play rugby or soccer. Ultimate is for geeks.
2. There are no after-game cheers, but they do have after-game contests like "Gibbon" or any game involving Cadbury's chocolate.
3. After practice you go to the pub.
4. After tournaments you go to the pub.
5. You dress nicely to go to the pub.
6. At the pub, you may engage in rowdy sing-along songs about beer.
7. If someone tosses a penny in your glass you must chug it to save the queen from drowning.
8. A disc holds three pints of beer.
9. Indoor Ultimate is common because winter lasts eight months of the year.
10. The English are great hecklers.

THE GERMANS

1. Most calls (foul, pick, brick) are in English.
2. Seventy-five percent of German players count the stall in German: "*Zähle eins, zwei, drei...*"
3. A huck is called *langes Teil;* a hammer is usually referred to as an overhead.
4. Force backhand or forehand is *links auf* ("left side open") or *rechts auf* ("right side open"), which is more precise when considering left-handed players.
5. The Germans like to throw hammers and strange passes to open space.
6. The most popular cities for Ultimate are Munich, Mainz, Cologne, and Berlin.
7. After the game people will embrace in a circle and mutter some very nice words about one another.
8. Be prepared to find yourself in a co-ed shower after play, much like the Netherlands, Switzerland, Austria, and the Czech Republic.

Games are easy to find in both Germany and Switzerland. In Bali they like bungee jumping. The Barcelona scene is particularly receptive to travelers who appreciate cheap red wine. Players in Venezuela and Colombia have watched all the best Ultimate videos on UltiVillage.com and are stoked when a North American comes to town.

HOW TO GET A HANDBLOCK
STU DOWNS

Stuffing a thrower requires as much footwork as handiwork.

1. As the handler pivots and extends, you must do so with him or her, moving your feet sideways and ready to reverse direction instantly. Don't waste time swinging your hands around wildly attempting to intimidate or you'll get broken like a stick.

2. If you spot a big windup, do not slide directly over or you will undoubtedly get smacked while simultaneously committing a foul. Instead, jump back and then over.

3. A successful block should be followed by the guttural scream "Package!" if in friendly company.

TOURNAMENTS

When traveling it's always fun to pick up with a new and strange team. The following tournaments are great opportunities for high-spirited international action (be aware that you may have to make arrangements in advance to play).

Hat Tournaments

Register as an individual for the following competitions:

- *Pie de la Cuesta* (sand and grass). Acapulco, Mexico, late January.
- *Bar do Peixe* (sand). Lisbon, Portugal, late June.
- *Sarnen Red Hat* (grass). Sarnen, Switzerland, late July.
- *Porró Open* (sand). Barcelona, Spain, early November.
- *Vietnam Hat*. HCMC, Vietnam, late December.
- *Bangkok Hat*. Bangkok, Thailand, late January.

Team Tournaments

Pick up with a team at:

- *Kaimana Klassik* (grass). Waimanalo, Oahu, Hawaii, mid-February.
- *Paganello* (sand). Rimini, Italy, Easter weekend.
- *Nusantara Cup* (grass). Bali, Indonesia, early April.
- *Tom's Tourney* (grass). Brugge, Belgium, early May.
- *Wonderful Copenhagen* (grass). Copenhagen, Denmark, early May.
- *Boracay Open* (sand). Boracay, Aklan, Philippines, early May.

TRAINING: CAN IT HAPPEN TO YOU?

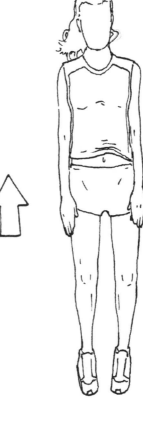

Repeat one hundred times in sets of four, twice a day for ten weeks.

Most people play Ultimate so they don't have to train. No one is going to pay you to practice. So why work so hard for so little in return? Ultimate isn't really about that, is it?

Unfortunately, since Ultimate began, some players have used training and conditioning to gain an unfair advantage. For them Ultimate is about sky-ing the opponent, getting open at will, winning challenges on the field. It's

PUNISHMENT AS TRAINING

IF YOU'RE NOT A PRIME PHYSICAL SPECIMEN, YOU MAY WANT TO AVOID THE FOLLOWING METHODS OF CONDITIONING:

1. Suicides
2. Running a snake
3. Leaping scissor kicks
4. Wind sprints
5. Running stairs (or hills)
6. Spinning
7. Jingle Jangles
8. Track workouts on an actual track
9. X-pattern multi-skill
10. Fifteen-Week Air Alert II course
11. Ten-minute Death
12. Anything in "sets"

very jock to be into such things. What about people who don't work out? Shouldn't they be able to win, too? Yes they should and yes they can.

Before you join a team, you should find out what the team regards as "playing condition." For some squads, workouts are optional. Others demand a rigid conditioning schedule with gratuitous practices and excessive running. Budget your time wisely if your team is big on training and be careful because regular conditioning may result in thinking of yourself as a serious athlete.

Note: If your team practices or has workouts three times a week or more, not including weekend tournaments, you'd better make the UPA Championships.

NONTRADITIONAL CONDITIONING

SOMETIMES ULTIMATE PLAYERS LIKE TO TRY NEW, UNORTHODOX TECHNIQUES. TO IMPROVE YOUR GAME, CONSIDER THE FOLLOWING:

1. Bikram yoga
2. Holistic speed training
3. Pilates
4. Envisioning
5. Fantasy Ultimate
6. Thai Stick
7. Confidence-building by crushing weaker teams

PLAYER TYPE:
GREENIE

The media stereotype of Ultimate players is that of hippies left over from the 1970s. This was never accurate, because hippies were less into sports and more into social revolutions, free love and acid. Ultimate players aren't generally concerned with such things.

Nonetheless, the spirit of the hippie carries on in two different types of Ultimate player: the **Mellow Greenie** and the **Activist Greenie**. Although both tend to be super-spirited, friendly, and outgoing, the Activist Greenie will become fiercely indignant over sociopolitical "issues" while the Mellow Greenie will sigh deeply when politics comes up in conversation.

All Greenie types conform to the liberal stereotype: They seek to defend the environment, slow global warming, save endangered species, fight the military-industrial complex, and stop eating meat. Joining an Ultimate team provides them with new and receptive teammates for forwarding MoveOn.org e-mails.

DISPOSITION

Mellow Greenies find the joys of the universe in the equilibrium of peaceful competition—coed of course. They prefer not to call fouls because calling fouls can mess up positive vibes. Mellow Greenies don't join traveling teams because that brings stress and stress is bad.

PSYCHOLOGY

Ultimate is often thought of as some sort of cliquey, cult-like phenomenon. This is due to the work of Activist Greenies, who combine the unbridled enthusiasm of socialism with the insecurities of the superego. They tend to create an environment where everyone is welcome to play—everyone who follows the unwritten rules, that is.

THE GREENIE

PROFESSION Nonprofit worker, government-sector worker, or college student. All three provide ample time for Ultimate.

SPIRIT OF THE GAME The Mellow Greenie is a true paragon of the Spirit of the Game. The Activist Greenie is the true enforcer of the Spirit of the Game.

HISTORY At one time there were longhaired pot-smoking unwashed hippies who played Ultimate, but that type became extinct in the 1980s. A true longhair these days would fall in the Oddball category.

LOCAL HANGOUTS You can find Greenies at the natural food store during the day, the laundromat-bar in the evenings, or an Arcade Fire show at night. Activist Greenies can also be identified by their handle during internet town hall meetings.

QUOTE "Ultimate is the only sport where players call their own rule infractions and the people are really nice. You should come play!"

STYLE NOTES Activist Greenies can usually be prompted to dress up in costume for the Saturday-night party. They also tend to like arts and crafts. Mellow Greenies are often followers of jam bands.

THE BIG GREEN BUS In 2005 a group of fifteen players from Dartmouth Ultimate converted a diesel-powered bus to run on used vegetable oils from deep-fryers. With the ability to pick up free fuel at diners across the nation, the big green bus toured for the entire summer promoting alternative fuels. The bus made sure to hit a tournament every weekend—to the delight of most Ultimate players, who consider themselves eco-friendly.

Interestingly, the Dartmouth team was composed of a mix of Greenie and Engineer types, as someone had to figure out how to make sure the engine didn't clog from all that fry grease.

RELATED PLAYER TYPES Outdoorsmen or **Outdoorswomen** are often forest service workers, hiking guides, or camping specialists. They can also work for the Peace Corps, Americorps, Doctors Without Borders, or Habitat for Humanity. Outdoorsmen appreciate living life day to day. They cannot survive long without fresh air and ample sun. Outdoorsmen may show up at a tournament unannounced. An Outdoorsman who has left his or her job will become a **Backpacker**, a subcategory of the **Oddball**.

THE ULTIMATE HIGH: HOW TO DEAL WITH YOUR ADDICTION

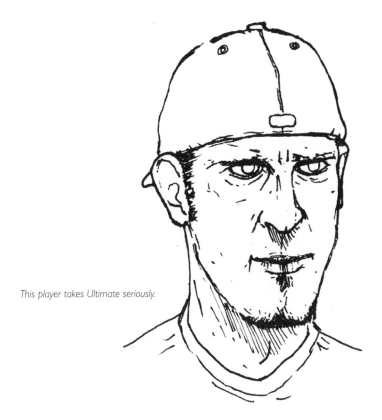

This player takes Ultimate seriously.

Ultimate isn't named such without good reason. Sure, many would-be players are turned off by its cult-like adherents and heathen reputation, but once you start playing it can be addictive and difficult to stop. Remember, college is a gateway drug.

In Ultimate, you get to do everything: run, jump, catch, throw, and dive. Your job is to shut down your opponent on defense, sky your defender on offense, and throw sweet passes all day long.

When you play Ultimate, the action is always on. You may begin to crave the action, your body desperately needing a layout and your mind filled with images of the game. You start to become dependent on completed hucks to satisfy urges, your life spiraling into one long endless summer of Ultimate. You may be in trouble.

SIGNS OF ULTIMATE ADDICTION

1. Perpetually skinned elbows and knees.
2. You own three or more pairs of cleats.
3. Your housemates are Ultimate players.
4. Your co-workers are Ultimate players.
5. You read rec.sport.disc daily.
6. Your significant other is an Ultimate player.
7. You consider returning to college for a completely unnecessary fifth year.
8. When you dream, you throw a perfect 60-yard hammer.
9. You challenge your thirty-two-year-old friends to Beer Pong.
10. League play on Mondays, pickup on Tuesdays, league on Wednesdays, pickup on Thursdays, travel on Fridays, tournaments on Saturdays and Sundays. Repeat for six months.

SOLUTIONS TO ULTIMATE ADDICTION

1. Get a job.
2. Switch your addiction to online poker.
3. Move to a small town in Mississippi, Arkansas, or Alaska.
4. Abstinence.
5. Reverential prayer to a higher power.
6. Get pregnant with twins.
7. Seconds and thirds from the tray of cannoli.
8. Win everything, retire, unretire, win everything you can again, retire. Repeat until knees wear out.

ULTIMATE IN POPULAR CULTURE

Killer.

Did you know that Ultimate has been a regular presence in popular culture since the 1970s? Check out these fun facts.

IN 1972 *The New York Times* attended the first intercollegiate Ultimate game between Rutgers and Princeton.

IN 1975 *Time* magazine profiled Ultimate, describing it as "a zany mixture of razzle-dazzle football, playground basketball and soccer."

IN THE 1979 cycling movie *Breaking Away*, the Cutters, a group of outsiders lead by Dennis Quaid, run over a disc that some frat boys at Indiana University had thrown in the street.

IN 1982 the movie *Tron* became a huge blockbuster. In one memorable sequence the star, Jeff Bridges, had to fight to survive by throwing and catching electrified killer discs.

IN THE LATE 1980s Ultimate was never seen in popular culture because the good life was all about beach volleyball, Oakley sunglasses, and Sunkist soda.

IN 1993 a game that looked like Ultimate aired in a Frosted Flakes commercial when Tony the Tiger made a great play by catching a disc in the end zone.

IN 1994, the college movie *PCU* starring Jeremy Piven, Jon Favreau, and George Clinton and the P-Funk All-Stars featured an Ultimate game between

HOW TO BOX OUT YOUR DEFENDER ON A FLOATY HUCK

VICTORINO BASQUIAT, EXPERT PLAYER

1. Run really fast to where the disc is arriving. If it floats or your defender is on your heels, you may have to box him/her out.

2. Jump. Time your jump so as to beat your defender. Never mind the box out, it will happen naturally as you read the disc.

3. If the throw was swilly and you needed to box out but didn't, and you failed to get the disc, then on the sidelines make sure to complain loudly how no one on your team can throw.

the all-female militant team the Womynists and the stoner team Jerry Town. The Womynists led 14-0 when Jerry Town brought in its superstar, a dog named Blotter, who caught the team's only goal.

IN THE LATE 1990s Ultimate was never seen in popular culture because snowboarding, skateboarding, and wakeboarding were totally rad.

IN 2000 Ultimate was part of a commercial for Speed Stick deodorant, by Mennen.

IN 2005, *Aqua Teen Hunger Force* rapper MC Chris's song "Eating's Not Cheating" contained the following lyric: "To everybody in high school who made fun of me because I was too asthmatic to play Ultimate Frisbee and I had to sit on the bench the whole time and read fucking books about Narnia, fuck you guys."

IN 2005 Michelob Ultra aired a beer commercial starring a guy and girl playing Ultimate. The girl scored a goal with a hot layout grab. Then the guy scored.

IN THE NOVEMBER 13, 2005, episode of *Family Guy*, Stewie Griffin says, "You know what I found out about college? That I am *so* all about Ultimate Frisbee."

IN 2006 Claritin, an allergy medication, aired a commercial featuring three Ultimate players. They play better with the medication because they can see the disc clearly. The commercial aired on all four major networks at once.

ON JUNE 10, 2006, ESPN's *Sportscenter* put a video of Beau Kittredge of Colorado jumping over a defender at number nine on its "Top Ten Plays of the Day." According to sources who saw the clip, ESPN anchor Stuart Scott said, "Open Southwest Regionals, Colorado versus San Diego, Colorado's Beau Kittridge... AND THE LAWD SAID, YOU GOTS TO RISE UP!!! BooYah! He must be the bus driver cuz he was takin' him to school. Holla."

IN APRIL 2009, the third-ranked University of Oregon men's team made national A.P. news when their season was cancelled by an uptight school administration after playing a "naked point" against their B team at sectionals.

PLAYER TYPE:
PARTIER

The Partier is an integral part of what makes Ultimate so shameless. Every sport has its fair share of social animals and unrepentant boozehounds. On game day, however, these sports are taken seriously by team squares (coaches, managers, owners, sportswriters, et cetera), who force upon the social player the need to be *chill*. In Ultimate, things are different. There are no coaches, managers, owners or sportswriters, and thus fewer restrictions.

The Partier has to be able to consume large amounts of alcohol, stay up ridiculously late, and still manage to *bring it* to the nine o'clock game the following morning. It's a tough task, but someone has to do it, and that someone is usually a college student.

THE PARTIER

More than half of all collegiate players fit into the Partier category. In Ultimate, playing with a hangover, while hindering one on the field of play, is still critical to the primary goal of the weekend. The primary goal of *every* weekend is to win as many contests (Ultimate, Flip Cup, Ro-Sham, Beirut, Hot Box, et cetera) as possible and maximize your fun.

AVERAGE HOURS OF SLEEP 4.5. The Partier can fall asleep in an instant, and he or she requires no frivolities like pillows, blankets, or clothes.

STAMINA High. A Partier can tolerate ruinous nighttime conditions and yet retain enough strength and energy to play competitively the next day.

STYLE It's the Partier that makes Ultimate unique. It's cool to dress up like a freakshow, and Partiers are often keen to do so. Many Partiers are first-class streakers who will get naked on any thin excuse. Rowdy cheers, land-sharking, human pyramids, table dancing, tabletopping, and other non-sense befitting kids with ADD is encouraged and exacerbated by the Partier. A good Partier appreciates all forms of anarchic fun. If all you're going to do is get wasted, you might as well play lacrosse.

QUOTE "Quarters? I'm in as soon as I finish Flip Cup."

RELATED PLAYER TYPES *The* **Tournament Slut** and **Frisbee Ho**. There are Partiers who like to hang out with their team, smoke two or three bowls, knock down a few pitchers, and pass out at 3 AM. And then there are Tournament Sluts—partiers who recognize that the best part of Ultimate is playing and partying with different teams as often as possible.

There are two or three tournaments every weekend in North America that welcome freelance players. Tournament Sluts are mercenaries who jump from team to team and party to party seeking an everlasting Ultimate fix.

Frisbee Hos are basically the same, except instead of jumping from tournament to tournament, they jump from one Ultimate relationship to another, and *then* from team to team and tournament to tournament.

HUCKS, SCOOBERS AND SWILLY CHUCKERS: A GLOSSARY OF ULTIMATE LINGO

TYPES OF THROWS

AIRBOUNCE: a backhand released with your thumb on the back of the disc, causing it to start low to the ground and then rise.

BACKHAND: the disc is gripped with the thumb on the topside of the disc and the fingers underneath for balance. The back of your hand faces the direction you are throwing. A good throw is made by snapping the wrist upon release. This is the most common throw in Ultimate.

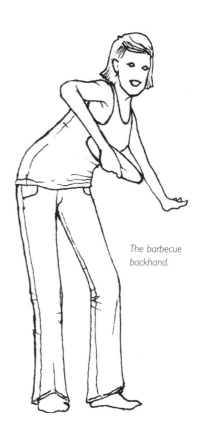

The barbecue backhand.

BARBECUE BACKHAND (also called **THE DAD**): a backhand throw by an inexperienced player who curls the disc inward and throws with his or her arm instead of the wrist. (*see illustration*)

BLADE (also called **KNIFE**): a throw that is released perpendicular to the ground and comes in perpendicular to the ground.

TWENTY-EIGHT NEAR-USELESS THROWS ON THE FIELD

THESE THROWS ARE FOR EXPERTS, SHOWBOATS, FREESTYLERS, SEAN LAING AND FLUTTER GUTS COMPETITORS ONLY.

The Chicken-Wing	The Jibba
Push pass	Nutmeg (also called Five-Hole)
Overhead Thumber	Behind-the-Back
Thumber huck	Airbounce
McFloogan	Flapjack
The Bowler	Biscuit
The Future	The Fireball
The Past	The Enterprise
Throw-of-Death	Triple Threat
Wheel-of-Death	High Plains Drifter
Overhand Wrist Flip	Low Plains Drifter
Sombrero	The Ox Driver
Olé	Intentional Double-Helix Hammer
Maitre D'	Any throw popularized by Sean Laing

CHICKEN-WING (also called **CORKSCREW**): a type of hammer with the disc in an upside-down backhand grip instead of the forehand grip; released to the side of the head and across the body.

DUMP PASS (also called **RESET**): a short pass of any kind, usually to a handler in the backfield to reposition the offense or reset the stall count.

FOREHAND (also called **FLICK, TWO-FINGER**): The disc is gripped with two fingers on its inside rim and the thumb gripped on the outside rim. Snapping your wrist forward completes the motion. The palm of your hand faces the direction you are throwing; opposite to the backhand.

GARBAGE: a throw that bounces off a person (or persons) and may be caught (**COLLECTING THE GARBAGE**) by an unintended receiver. A garbage pass is usually the result of a swilly throw.

GRASS BURNER: a low throw that skims the field. Can also refer to the stoner on your team.

HAMMER (also called **TOPPER, BOWL, OVERHEAD**): a common throw released with a forehand grip over your head that comes in upside down to the receiver.

HIGH RELEASE: typically, a backhand throw held high and released over the defender's shoulder.

A scoober.

HONEY PASS: a pass thrown between an acknowledged couple on the team.

HOSPITAL PASS: a high floating pass that has the effect of bringing two or more players together into a collision when they go for the disc. Not ideal for players, but welcomed by sideline hecklers.

HUCK (also called **DEEP LOOK, CRANK, RIP, BOMB**): a disc thrown long and deep, usually to the end zone. Can also be used as a verb, **TO HUCK.**

INSIDE-OUT (also called **IO**): a throw that starts off crossing the parallel plane between the thrower and receiver. It is the opposite of most throws, which are **OUTSIDE-IN** and start outside the parallel plane of the thrower's release.

NUTMEG: a throw between the defender's legs.

OLÉ: a short-distance high-release pass over the defender's head.

PUSH PASS: a near-spinless short throw, released by rolling the disc off the fingers or palm.

SCOOBER: a forehand-grip throw with a chopping motion across the thrower's body, released over the defender's head, usually to the breakmark side. (*see illustration*)

SWILL: a terrible pass, usually a huck, that floats or heads toward an unintended target or location.

THUMBER: any throw with the thumb gripping the inside lip of the disc.

EIGHTEEN EXPRESSIONS TO DESCRIBE HOW YOUR TEAM WAS SOUNDLY DEFEATED

SOMETIMES THE GAME ISN'T EVEN CLOSE.
"OH BOY, WE GOT _____ LAST GAME, 15-3."

Crushed	Rolled	Slaughtered
Killed	Destroyed	Waxed
Plastered	Hosed	Spanked
Schooled	Shredded	Pounded
Taken out back	Murdered	Bageled
Served	Tooled	Blown out

TYPES OF PLAYERS

AGGRO: taken from *aggressive*. Used to refer to a particularly hotheaded player or team.

BLACK HOLE: a player on your team whom you don't want to have the disc, because you'll probably never see it again.

CAG: a handler reset position.

CUTTER: in a horizontal stack, cutters line up downfield and make in and out cuts. In a vertical stack, deeps and mids are sometimes called cutters.

DEEP (also called **LONG**): deeps are a team's desired scorers who make distance cuts into the end zone.

FLUFFER: any player who makes another player look good.

HACK: (*noun*) a person who fouls often. (*verb*) **TO HACK:** hitting a person's hand or body.

HANDLER: (also called **SHORT**): handlers are the team's primary throwers and distributors of the disc. They can dictate the flow of the offense; some are known as good huckers.

MIDDLE (also called **MID**): in a vertical stack, a middle traditionally lines up in the middle of the stack, cutting back to the handlers and sometimes to the end zone in a half-field set.

MIDDLE-MIDDLE: the center player in the cup formation of a zone defense.

NIGHTMARE: see **BLACK HOLE** or **TURNOVER MACHINE**.

POACHER: a player who doesn't guard his or her person and instead looks to step into the throwing lanes to make a defensive play.

ROCKSTAR: a very good player.

SOLID: used to describe a consistently good player who makes few mistakes.

SWILLY CHUCKER: a player who insists on always hucking the disc long, usually for turnovers.

TURNOVER MACHINE: a player who consistently throws the disc away.

ON THE FIELD

BAIL-OUT THROW: a throw made on a high stall count to avoid losing possession.

BIFF, GAK: when the disc bounces off the hands or chest. See also DROPSIES. (*see illustration*)

BREAK: (*noun*) (1) when the defense scores a goal on an offensive point. (2) a throw to the side of the field against or opposite to the force. (*verb*) TO BREAK means to throw a pass (a BREAKMARK) against the marker's force side.

Biff, gak and dropsy.

BOOKENDS (also called DOUBLE HAPPINESS): a successful D and subsequent score by the same player.

BOWLING ALLEY: an in-cut up the line and toward the thrower for long distance.

CALLAHAN: (1) a defensive catch in the starting end zone of the offense (resulting in a goal) is called a CALLAHAN GOAL. (2) The Player of the Year award in college is called the CALLAHAN AWARD, named for former player Henry Callahan.

CHILLY: to be chill on offense means to not get overly amped trying to score quickly.

CLAM: a type of zone defense.

CONSERVATION OF GREATNESS: the phenomenon that occurs when a great play (for example, a sick layout D) exhausts a player's well of talent, causing that same player to follow up the great play with a turnover (usually a throwaway).

HOW TO THROW A SCOOBER 30 YARDS FOR A GOAL

KIRK SAVAGE

This throw is not for everyone, but if you think it is for you:

1. Hold the disc in both hands and look like you might throw a backhand.

2. Wait for your teammate to cut to the break side. You should only use the scoober to throw breakmarks.

3. Flip the disc upside down. Release the disc high and past your defender's head. Make sure to lead your teammate by aiming the disc to float back towards your receiver.

4. Go for it. No guts, no glory—but do not turn this throw over. You must be near 100% completion with the scoober or your teammates will be upset, and rightly so.

CUP: usually three or more defenders who surround the thrower in a zone defense.

D (short for **DEFENSE**): (1) a defensive block or defensive catch. (2) playing defense.

DEFENSIVE SKIRT: when a male player makes a good play, he can be awarded the defensive skirt to be worn during the game.

DROPPING BUCKETS (also called **MAKING IT RAIN**): scoring points.

DROPSIES: a condition that causes a player or team to drop an easy pass.

FLAT: generally, the horizontally open side of the field.

FORCE: defensive positioning of the marker and the downfield defense to a particular side or direction. There are five primary forces: **FOREHAND, BACKHAND, FORCE MIDDLE, FORCE SIDELINES,** and **STRAIGHT-UP.**

FOREPLAY: the phenomenon of throwing exclusively to the player you have a crush on.

GRATUITOUS: usually said of an unnecessary layout.

THE GREATEST: a completed pass whereby a player with good presence of mind, seeing that the disc is going out of bounds with no chance of being caught in bounds, will leap from in bounds, catch the disc in midair and throw the disc in a single motion back in bounds for a completion.

HANDBLOCK and **FOOTBLOCK** (also called **POINT BLOCK, STUFF, FLAPJACK**): similar to shot blocking in basketball, a handblock or footblock occurs when blocking (or stuffing) a just-released disc while on the mark.

HOW TO PLAY MIDDLE-MIDDLE IN A ZONE D

STU DOWNS

The middle-middle is undoubtedly the best position in a zone, the only one surrounded on all sides by teammates.

1. Your teammates will let you know where cutters are headed and can cover your slack when you bid. This allows you to be risky, and often glorious.
2. Puma-like reflexes and a willingness to fly are key to denying passage through the middle of the cup. Always be ready to lunge or dive, even on a fake.
3. Keep your feet and arms active. Shifting left and right like you're receiving a serve in tennis disturbs a thrower intent on dicing you up; it makes you unpredictable and usually discourages the attempt.

HIBACHI HARI-KARI: said when a player on your team scores a lot of points in one game and then buries your team the next. In reference to Gil Arenas.

HORIZONTAL O or **H-STACK:** an offensive setup where the players line up perpendicular to the direction of play.

LAYOUT (also called **HO, HORIZONTAL, BID, DIVE**): diving for the disc on offense or defense is called a layout. You can get a layout **GRAB**, get a layout **D BLOCK**, or miss the disc, which is commonly called a **BID**.

LOOK OFF: when the thrower does not throw the disc to an open receiver.

MAC: an acronym that stands for "midair correction." It refers to a disc that is tipped in flight but continues, usually at a different trajectory.

(TO) MARK: guarding your person when he or she has the disc in hand.

O (short for **OFFENSE**): offense or an offensive line.

PANCAKE: catching the disc with two hands, one underneath and one on top of the disc.

PICK: a violation by intentionally or unintentionally blocking a defender from guarding his or her person.

PULL: the opening throw-off to start a point.

(TO) ROACH: burning your defender and getting open.

(TO) ROACH THE POACH: to burn the player poaching on you.

SAFETY MEETING: calling in teammates to huddle for an herbage session.

HOW TO THROW AN INSIDE-OUT FOREHAND

BECCA TUCKER

1. Hold the disc so that the far edge is tilted down.
2. Lean down so that the elbow of your throwing hand is below your knee.
3. Release at a slight upward angle so that the disc will cross your body and curve back to the receiver.

SAVAGE: (*noun*) playing a game or tournament with the minimum number of players, usually seven. (*verb*) to intentionally leave someone behind on a road trip.

(TO) SKY: outjumping your competition to get to the disc first.

(TO) SPIKE: intentionally throwing the disc into the ground after a score. Can also refer to any type of pronounced action with the disc after a score (throwing it in the air, rolling it on the ground, using it as a serving platter for a bohemian cocktail party). A spike is sometimes considered taunting the opposing team.

STALL COUNT: the amount of time a thrower has to release the disc, usually ten seconds, counted out by the marker.

THE STUPIDEST: contra-positive to the Greatest. When a player leaps from in bounds for a Greatest attempt, flips the disc to the middle of the field for an incompletion, and then lands in bounds, meaning the Greatest need not have been attempted in the first place.

SQUIRRELLY: said when a handler or middle makes a series of fairly useless short cuts in a jittery fashion.

SWILLY: terrible or crappy.

TOAST: when the offensive player cuts one direction and the defender cuts the other, leaving the offensive player wide open.

(TO) TURF: throwing a pass into the ground.

VERTICAL STACK: an offensive setup with players lined up parallel to the direction of play.

ZONE: a type of defense (which is countered by the offense) where players guard areas of the field instead of individual players. There are many zone varieties for both offense and defense.

NINE EXPRESSIONS FOR GETTING BEAT ONE-ON-ONE

IT HAPPENS TO EVERYONE: THE PERSON YOU ARE GUARDING IS QUICKER, FASTER, SMARTER AND TALLER THAN YOU. WHEN YOU GET BEAT, YOU GET _____ .

Burned	Roasted	Roached
Toasted	Scorched	Skyed
D'ed up	Shut down	Schooled

OFF THE FIELD

(TO) BAIL: skipping out on a tournament or ditching a team.

FANTASY ULTIMATE: like fantasy baseball; picking players on the field for their statistics and keeping a running tally.

KARMA: used to refer to a good play or bad play that works in conjunction with the perceived good or bad spirit a player possesses.

STREET DISC: a scraped-up disc, useless for the playing field but perfect for the parking lot.

TIRAMISU: a delightful Italian dessert pastry invented in the 1970s whose name means "pick-me-up" or in Italian, "makes-a-me-a-happy!" Tiramisu consists of: spongey biscuits, espresso coffee, mascarpone cheese, eggs, cream, sugar, Marsala wine, cocoa, and rum.

VIRGIN PLASTIC: a new, unused disc.

VITAMIN I: ibuprofen.

WINNING THE PARTY: being the last person(s) to stay up partying at a tournament.

QUIZ: WHAT IS YOUR ULTIMATE APTITUDE?

Take this short quiz to test your aptitude for all things Ultimate. The answers appear on p. 134.

1 In Fantasy Ultimate, how many points do you get when your positive pick throws a hammer for a score? If your negative pick calls a time-out?

2 If you're attending the Mardi Gras tournament in Baton Rouge, Louisiana, what microbrew might you be drinking?

3 What university won the 2006 national championship in football, men's basketball, and men's Ultimate?

4 How many fouls do you get in the UPA Championship Series before fouling out?

5 The Stanford Women's team and Yale Men's team share the same name. What is it?

6 What are Speed TDs?

7 Who plays the best Ultimate? East Coast or West Coast?

8 Identify at least two teams named for a rap, hip-hop, or funk song.

9 A defensive catch in the opponent's end zone is called a what?

10 What is a landshark?

11 What Hollywood producer made *Commando, Richie Rich,* and *Ghost Ship*?

12 What do you get when you win the UPA College Championships?

13 What are the dimensions of the end zone in standard Ultimate?

14 What does *WFDF* stand for?

15 What Ultimate-like game is played by throwing a disc through a large semicircular hoop attached to the ground?

ABOUT THE AUTHOR

Tony was christened with the name Pasquale Anthony at an early age in South Bend, Indiana. He has been playing Ultimate since 1988 and writing about it since 1997. In the grown-up world he operates as a writer, cinematographer, location sound man, hand model and hellion. He lives in Brooklyn, New York, and/or somewhere out West.

ABOUT THE ILLUSTRATOR

Cade is an artist and designer from Portland, Maine. He loves art, music, coffee, Ultimate and micron archival pens. He resides in Boston, Massachusetts. Cade would like to thank Bob Kelly, Jesse B, Meredith, Nano for the drafting table, and his parents for everything else.

CONTRIBUTORS

GWEN AMBLER—How to Throw Completed Hucks
UPA College champion with Stanford Superfly, three-time UPA Club champion with San Francisco Fury, founder of *Inside College Ultimate* (www.icultimate.com).

KEITH ASPINALL—How to Run a Successful Tournament
Director of Tempe, Arizona's New Year Fest since 2001. New Year Fest is one of the country's most popular and longest-running tournaments.

STU DOWNS—How to Get a Handblock, How to Play Middle-Middle in a Zone D Long-time leader of Atlanta's Chain Lightning, who once lost 16 straight games at the UPA Club Championships. Former "Mr. Frisbee" (1988).

DOMINIQUE FONTENETTE—How to Sky a Taller Player
1997 Callahan Winner. Four-time UPA Club champion with San Francisco Fury and Boston Lady Godiva. UPA College champion with Stanford Superfly. World Games champion with Team USA.

KATEY FORTH—How to Get a Layout D Block
Former captain of six-time Paganello champions London Bliss, founder of Houston Showdown, member of Great Britain Nationals team since 1996.

MIKE GRANT—How to Play With Your Off-Hand
Three-time UPA Club champion with Vancouver Furious George. Played and won the 2004 World Club Ultimate Championships with his left hand after dislocating his right elbow.

DAN HEIJMEN—How to Captain a College Team
2007 Callahan winner. Captain of the 2007 UPA College champion University of Wisconsin Hodags.

SEAN MCCALL—How to Put on a Good Mark
Founder and captain of Houston Doublewide and five-time Paganello champions Houston No Tsu Oh.

JIM PARINELLA—How to Get Open
Former captain and six-time UPA Club champion with Boston Death or Glory. Co-writer of *Ultimate: Techniques & Tactics*.

KIRK SAVAGE—How to Throw a Scoober 30 Yards for a Goal
Three-time UPA Club Open champion with Vancouver Furious George. World
Games champion with Team Canada.

CHASE SPARLING-BECKLEY—How to Catch a Blade in Traffic
UPA College champion with Carleton College, three-time UPA Club champion
with Seattle Sockeye, World Games champion with Team USA, 2009 UPA Mixed
champion with Axis of C'ville. Caught game-winning blade at double-game point
for Sockeye in UPA Club Open finals 2004.

BECCA TUCKER—How to Throw an Inside-Out Forehand
Captain of New York Ambush '06-'07. Player with Women's Team USA at 2007
World Beach Ultimate Championships in Brazil. Most likely to send weed to the
UPA headquarters and then call the cops.

SCOBEL WIGGINS—How to Shoot Good Ultimate Pictures
Official photographer for numerous UPA Club and College Championships, as
well as tournaments in the Northwest.

*Victorino Basquiat
in a flutter guts match.*

Bold page numbers indicate illustrations and/or awesomeness.

M

N

O

P

Q

R

ANSWERS TO QUIZ, P. 124

1: PLUS FOUR; ZEROES YOUR SCORE.
2: ABITA TURBODOG.
3: UNIVERSITY OF FLORIDA.
4: UNLIMITED.
5: SUPERFLY.
6: NIKE CLEATS.
7: THE ANSWER DEPENDS ON WHERE YOU'RE FROM.
8: SUPERFLY, ATOMIC DOGS, CRUNK JUICE, FRESH & CLEAN; THERE ARE OTHERS.
9: CALLAHAN GOAL.
10: A NAKED PERSON WITH A DISC LODGED BETWEEN HIS/HER BUTT CHEEKS CARRIED AROUND BY A GROUP OF PEOPLE. IT'S ALSO A NIKE CLEAT.
11: JOEL SILVER.
12: A GOLD-PLATED MEDAL AND PERMANENT GLORY.
13: FORTY YARDS WIDE AND 25 YARDS DEEP.
14: WORLD FLYING DISC FEDERATION.
15: GOALTIMATE OR DISC HOOPS.

SCORING

14-15: ELITE.   10-13: STARTING 7   .5-9: SOPHOMORE.   0-4: NEWBIE.